THE STUDENT PASTA COOK BOOK

First published in Great Britain in 1993
by Collins & Brown Limited
Letts of London House
Great Eastern Wharf
Parkgate Road
London SW11 4NQ

1 3 5 7 9 8 6 4 2

British Library Cataloguing-in-Publication Data:
A catalogue record for this book
is available from the British Library.

ISBN 1 85585 174 1

Conceived, edited and designed by Collins & Brown Limited

Editor: Elfreda Powell

Art Director: Roger Bristow

Designed by: Claire Graham

Typeset by Falcon Graphic Art Ltd
Printed and bound in
Finland by WSOY

THE STUDENT PASTA COOKBOOK

Eating well without mixer, microwave or money

Sarah Freeman

• ACKNOWLEDGEMENTS •

As with the previous *Student Cook Books*, I have been helped in compiling this by many people, and I am very grateful to them all. In particular, I want to thank Polly Freeman for organizing a constantly changing team of student testers; Amy Spurling for testing and reporting on a large number of recipes with exceptional flair; and Alex Freeman for his assistance at every stage in their progress. I also owe a considerable debt to Carla Tomasi, principal of the cookery school, Turnaround Cooks; to the cookery demonstrator Kumud Shah; and also to Supasri Gilbert, David Eyre and to the writer Yan-Kit So, both for her inspirational books and her personal kindness.

On the literary front, Mandy Greenfield and Sarah Hoggett, at Collins & Brown, have earned my special gratitude, not only for editorial help and advice, but also for their patience, encouragement and humour, which have added enormously to my enjoyment in writing the book.

Others who deserve thanks are Elfreda Powell, Pasta Foods, J. Sainsbury PLC, the Ministry of Food, and finally my long-suffering husband (although he says that he has not suffered), who for over a year has lived on an almost continuous diet of pasta and noodles (and has proved the point that I have made elsewhere that, even if eaten in quite large quantities, pasta should not cause people to put on weight).

• CONTENTS •

• Introduction •

The idea for this series of books came from a group of students who wanted to be able to cook and eat really well despite living on grants and lack of previous experience in the kitchen. After some discussion, it was agreed that besides being cheap and straightforward, the recipes should call mainly for ingredients available at supermarkets; that no more than minimal kitchen equipment should be assumed; and that in general dishes should be restricted to main-course items, since unless they were giving dinner-parties, people did not have time to prepare first courses or puddings.

In the first two books (*The Student Cook Book* and *The Student Vegetarian Cook Book*), I gave a selection of dishes of various types and ethnic origin; however, as pasta and noodles fulfil the needs specified by the students particularly well, a complete book on them was an obvious idea. *The Student Pasta Cook Book* follows almost the same pattern as its predecessors, since the same conditions are observed and the book divided in much the same way: there are recipes for soups (all suitable for main courses); a wide selection of sauces to go with pasta; stir-fried and several Indian dishes; salads; and, as before, a chapter on ideas for when you are really broke. This time, I have added a chapter for when you are really in a hurry. The book opens with a section on pasta itself, including recipes for making your own, which is far easier than most people think, and enables you to make dishes such as ravioli and cannelloni of real distinction and individuality.

Every recipe has been tested by a team of students and any which were not considered sufficiently delicious or found too time-consuming or expensive omitted. The fact that some of the directions are rather long does not mean that the dishes are difficult, but simply that I have explained every step in detail for those without experience in the kitchen. In some cases (notably recipes for fried noodles) I have also given alternative methods of cooking.

All the items of cookery equipment needed have been listed

with each recipe so that you can see at a glance if there is anything that you will have to borrow or improvise. Despite an inevitable Italian, or in the case of noodles, Chinese influence, I have avoided any specialist items which are not widely available and relatively cheap. Finally, I should like to stress that, in the interests of both health and gastronomy, all the ingredients given are fresh except for one or two preserved products such as olives and tinned Italian tomatoes.

• INGREDIENTS •

Vegetables, Herbs, and Spices: The operative word here is 'fresh'. I have described how to judge when vegetables are fresh and given any other relevant information about them at the head of the recipes; similarly, I have commented on particular herbs where necessary. I know that fresh herbs are expensive and often difficult to buy; unfortunately, however, dried ones (with the exception of oregano) are no substitute, since they seldom have much flavour. To minimize the problem, I have used herbs only occasionally, where they really count, but suggest (as I already have in the previous two books) that the best idea is to grow your own. The ones needed in this book are parsley, thyme, chives, basil, and rosemary, all of which except the last can be kept in pots on the window-sill. The first three are hardy and will grow easily; basil is killed by cold and, as an annual, will die in the winter anyway, but if you buy a plant in the spring and bring it indoors at night it should flourish until the following autumn.

Spices similarly lose much of their flavour and character after being ground. For this reason (except for one or two, which cannot be pulverized at home) I have assumed that you will buy them whole and crush them yourself just before use.

Chillies: Two points need to be made about chillies, which I have used in a number of recipes, usually only in sufficient quantity to add zest or depth of flavour rather than heat. One is that there are many different kinds, and they vary considerably in strength. In general, red are hotter than green; long, pod-shaped ones hotter than pepper-shaped; and small, hotter than large (which means that using a small one when you want a mild result is a mistake); there is also a round variety called Scotch Bonnet which is particularly fiery.

The second point is that the chemical which makes them hot may cause your hands to smart after preparing them: it will also affect your eyes if you touch them, the knife, and other articles with which it comes into contact. I have therefore warned against rubbing your eyes and included directions for washing your hands directly after handling chillies wherever they occur.

Pepper: Anyone who has been to an Italian restaurant will have noticed the waiter who offers to grind fresh pepper from an enormous pepper-mill over your pasta. Pepper counts as a spice and, like others, has far more taste when freshly ground. If you have no pepper-mill and sufficient energy, you can crush peppercorns with a pestle and mortar; in any case, choose black rather than white.

Salt: Freshly ground sea-salt rather than the usual powdered table-salt will add freshness and subtlety to everything you cook. As you are unlikely to have a salt-mill, I recommend Malden sea-salt, which has a gentle, almost herb-like taste and comes in flakes: you can use it as it is for cooking or crush it with the back of a spoon for serving at table.

Oil: Although in the previous book I specified olive oil for pasta and some other dishes, I did not like to draw attention to it because of its cost. All I can say here is that I always use it for pasta (as opposed to noodle) dishes and all the pasta recipes have been tested with it. There are several qualities: 'Extra Virgin' comes from the first pressing of the olives and has the strongest taste; 'Virgin' is the next quality down, and 'Pure' the cheapest. Pure is perfectly adequate for cooking purposes and with some dishes definitely the most suitable because its flavour is relatively discreet. At the time of going to press, it costs about £1.80p–£2 for 500 ml/nearly a pint. Partly to help to offset this, I have given as little as is consistent with good results and easy cooking throughout: most of the sauces call for only a tablespoonful, which means that a 500-ml bottle will last about a month. If you still cannot afford it, use sunflower oil.

For stir-fried dishes (where rather more oil is needed), I recommend groundnut oil, which costs 80–90p for 500 ml.

Cheese: The other relatively expensive item needed for pasta dishes is Italian Parmesan or pecorino cheese, for which there really is no substitute. Parmesan is subtler but, in the same way as spices, loses its flavour quickly after grating. If you use it, buy it in a block and grate it freshly for each occasion. Pecorino keeps its flavour better and is now sold in ready-grated form in some supermarkets: when you want ready-grated cheese, I strongly recommend it instead of Parmesan (I use it myself). If you buy it in a block, you may find that there is a choice of several varieties: the kind needed for sprinkling on pasta is pecorino Romano.

• THE STORE-CUPBOARD •

One of the especial advantages of pasta and noodles is that you can make a wide variety of dishes without having to buy more than one or two ingredients if you keep a few basic items in the house. Apart from a supply of pasta and noodles themselves, I suggest that you stock your cupboard with a couple of tins of peeled plum tomatoes, a tin of olives in brine, and a tin of tuna fish in brine; in addition, keep a spare tube of tomato purée, a spare canister of pecorino, dried chillies and oregano, bottles of olive and groundnut oil and dark and light soy sauce, and a bag of plain flour (for making your own pasta).

If at any time you are feeling rich, you might add a 25 g/1 oz packet of porcini (dried mushrooms), which will cost 80–90p, a jar of sun-dried tomatoes (the cheapest I have been able to find are about £1.40p for 285 g), and, for one or two particularly special noodle dishes, Amontillado sherry, most of which you can drink, since you need only a very little for cooking.

The fresh items which you will constantly need, besides

cheese, are onions and garlic, which will keep for several weeks, plus celery, tomatoes, and root ginger.

• NUTRITION •

Part of the current tremendous popularity of pasta stems from its reputation for being healthy, which is because dishes based on it contain more starch and less saturated fat than the average meal centred on meat. I have said more about fats and other constituents of food at the back of the book, where I have also given a table of food values; meanwhile, it is certainly true that a dish of pasta or noodles will provide you with a very well-balanced meal so long as it includes cheese and/or another high-protein ingredient such as meat, fish, beans, or tofu. And it will be even better balanced if you follow it with a simple salad or fresh fruit.

A rather different issue is whether pasta and noodles are particularly fattening, as is sometimes supposed. In themselves, I assure you that they are not, since they contain only flour, with or without eggs; the sauces which go with pasta, however, may be made with large amounts of oil, which accounts for pasta-lovers who put on weight. Since, as I have already stressed, the sauces in this book are made with the minimum practicable quantity, you have nothing to worry about on this score.

• EQUIPMENT •

I have taken it for granted that you will have the following: cooker and refrigerator; saucepans, including a large one for boiling pasta; a wok or frying-pan (but not both); scales, pestle and mortar, colander, sieve, bowls, knives, and spoons. I have not assumed that the saucepans will have lids, since saucepan-lids are expensive extras; where a covered pan is needed, it has been listed with the ingredients for the recipe.

In many instances, you can manage without scales: weights can be assessed from packets and a tablespoon used as an approximate measure for flour and sugar (1 level tablespoonful of sugar or 2 of flour = 25 g/1 oz). You can similarly measure liquid with milk-bottles or mugs (1 average mug = 300 ml/

1/2 pint). However, since it helps very much to start with a precise amount of flour when making pasta, I would say that for this purpose scales are necessary.

Pestles and mortars are expensive but I can think of no satisfactory alternative for crushing spices and herbs. If it is any consolation, once bought, they will last a lifetime.

Most of the dishes in this book are cooked on the hob rather than in the oven, and where you do need the oven, it will not matter if it is slightly inaccurate. However, if you think that it may be too hot, put your dish near the bottom, where it will be coolest; if it seems too cool, place it near the top. (This will not apply if the oven is fan-assisted.) Keep an eye on large dishes in particular, and if they show signs of burning at the back, turn them round.

• STORAGE AND HYGIENE •

Meat, fish, and all dairy produce except eggs should be stored in the refrigerator as soon as possible after purchase. Cut herbs and most vegetables should also be stored in the refrigerator: the chief exceptions are onions, garlic, tomatoes if you are leaving them to ripen for sauce, and all but new potatoes (small new potatoes should be kept chilled). Opened canisters of grated cheese will retain their flavour better if kept chilled; opened bottles of oyster sauce should be kept in the refrigerator. Eggs should not be chilled but stored somewhere cool.

All items stored in the refrigerator, including vegetables, should be wrapped or covered. Put cheese and other dairy products, cooked items, and fresh pasta near the top, and uncooked meat, fish, and vegetables near the bottom. Meat and cheese should be used by or before their sell-by dates, but in general meat keeps for three days; bacon for a week; fish for one day, although it is preferable to cook it as soon as you buy it; cooked dishes, one day; uncooked fresh pasta, two days; fresh herbs and vegetables (on average), two days. Take care not to let packages in the refrigerator leak; clean it out once a week.

Flour, dried pasta, sugar, spices, and other dry groceries, plus onions and garlic should be stored somewhere cool. Onions and garlic will keep for two or three weeks; for other items, you should check the best-before date to ascertain how long they will keep.

Wash your hands before starting to cook, after handling raw eggs, meat, or other fresh produce, and in particular before kneading or rolling dough or preparing salads.

• PREPARATION AND COOKING •

I have given complete directions for every process with the recipes except those listed below, which recur constantly throughout the book.

To chop onions: Cut in half lengthwise. Place the flat (cut) side on the chopping surface, and cross-chop.

To chop parsley: Squeeze into a tight bunch after washing and drying, and slice across.

To skin tomatoes: Immerse in boiling water for 30 seconds; drain, and if too hot to handle, rinse in cold water. Unless they are hard and underripe, the skin will then peel off easily.

To simmer: This means to cook in water which is just on the point of boiling. The top should move or bubble very slightly but not vigorously. To achieve the right heat calls for careful adjustment; if the item is to be covered, you also have to allow for the fact that adding a lid will raise the temperature slightly.

Vegetables: In order to retain as much as possible of their vitamin content, do not cut them up until just before use. Boil them in the minimum of water, and when possible re-use the water, e.g. for soups.

Eggs: These should be washed before use in case pieces of shell, which could cause contamination, fall into their contents. To crack them cleanly, tap sharply on the edge of a cup or bowl.

• A Note on Different Types • of Pasta and Noodles

The extraordinary elasticity of dough (which is due to the reaction of gluten with hydrogen) seems first to have been exploited by the Chinese, who were making noodles at least 1,500, if not 3,000 years ago. When and how the idea became known in Italy is uncertain: it used to be claimed that it was introduced by Marco Polo, but in fact the Italians had been making some form of pasta for a considerable time before he returned from his travels.

CHINESE NOODLES are traditionally pulled rather than rolled: pulling them is a spectacular procedure which is well worth watching if you have the chance. As follows from this, their typical form is as strings rather than hollow pipes; nor are short shapes customary. Not only wheat but other available flours are used to make them, notably rice and mung bean, which is made into so-called 'CELLOPHANE' NOODLES. The Japanese also make noodles from yam.

As with Italian egg pasta, Chinese egg and rice noodles are best when freshly made; in this country, however, fresh noodles can only be bought at good Chinese stores. Even dried rice ones are relatively difficult to find: a few supermarkets stock them, but in general choice is limited to one or two brands of dried egg noodle. When buying egg noodles, choose Chinese-made when available.

There is a bewildering variety of pasta available. Pasta made without eggs, i.e. from flour and/or semolina and water, which is known as 'dry' pasta (*pasta secca*), is usually factory-made and extruded into pipes or shapes. The best-known kinds are probably SPAGHETTI, MACARONI, and CONCHIGLIE (shells). However, there are also SPAGHETTINI and VERMICELLI, which are finer than spaghetti, and BUCATINI, which is thicker. Besides macaroni there are RIGATONI, which are larger and have a ribbed surface; BOMBALOTTI, which are larger and concave; and ribbed or plain PENNE, which are diagonally cut. Shapes include DITALI (thimbles), FARFALLE (butterflies), and FUSILLI (coils). There are

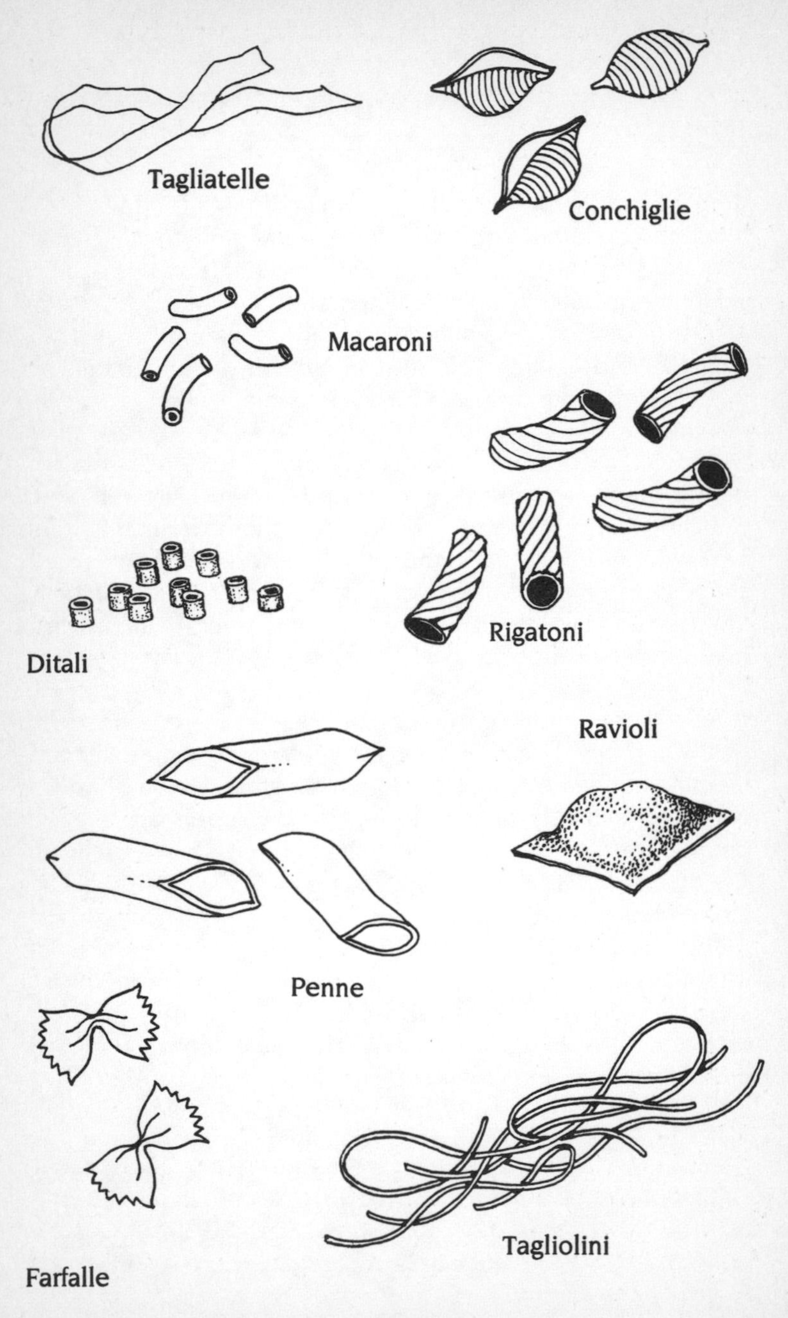
Tagliatelle
Conchiglie
Macaroni
Rigatoni
Ditali
Ravioli
Penne
Farfalle
Tagliolini

many others, and new ones are constantly being invented – the design of a new shape being a matter not of fancy but expertise, since form and texture serve particular purposes. Shells, for instance, catch sauce or soup inside; a ribbed surface is better adapted to holding sauce than a plain one; twists or coils expose a wider surface area than straight pipes. Similarly, different thicknesses of pipe suit differing types and textures of sauce.

To achieve the hard, satisfying 'bite', which is its particular quality, eggless pasta is (or should be) made of durum flour, or partly or entirely of semolina, both of which have a high gluten content. Although extrusion and drying also play their part, quality of flour is the most important factor in distinguishing very good, expensive pastas from the more ordinary kinds (and some top-quality brands can cost four or five times the average supermarket price). When choosing pasta, check on the packet to ensure that it is made from durum flour. Further advice on buying is difficult to give because, while I would recommend Italian brands, many British-labelled products are in fact made in Italy by Italian firms. Without being specific, which is dangerous because the marketing situation changes rapidly, I can only suggest that you try different products, including different types of pasta under the same label, until you can identify those that you like best.

Egg pasta, part of the character of which is the taste of the eggs, is supposed to be tender rather than hard (though it should still have 'bite') and, correspondingly, is made of soft flour. Although exceptions such as egg vermicelli and CAPRICCIOSA, a noodle made from fine semolina and egg, are available, in general eggs are used for ribbon pasta, stuffed pasta shapes and CANNELLONI, and LASAGNE. Ribbon pasta includes TAGLIOLINI (or TAGLIARINI), FETTUCINE and TAGLIATELLE. Shapes for stuffed pasta can be square (RAVIOLI), semi-circular (ANOLINI), or triangular (PANSOTI); there are also CAPPELLETTI (little hats) and TORTELLINI or TORTELLONI, which also look like hats.

The equivalent of top-quality *pasta secca* is freshly made egg pasta, which is becoming more readily available in pasta shops and supermarkets, at about three times the cost of dried pasta. But it can be made successfully at home for the price of an egg per serving plus flour.

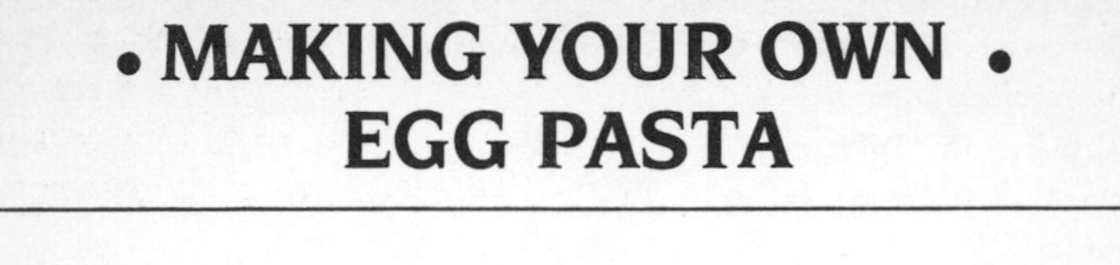

• MAKING YOUR OWN • EGG PASTA

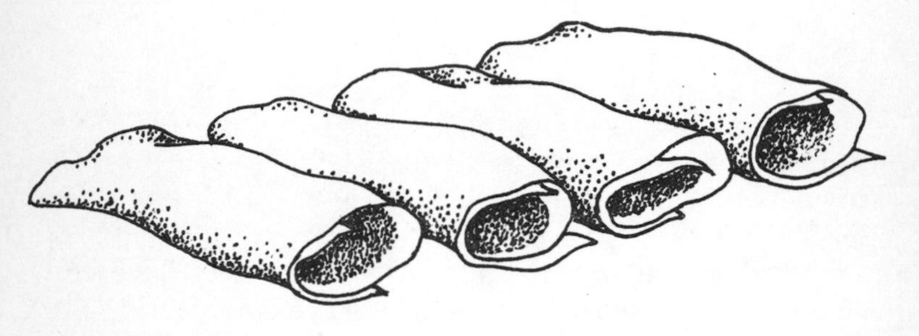

Pasta is much easier to handle than pastry, in that the dough does not crumble, nor is it liable to stick if it becomes too warm. Also, unlike bread, you do not have to wait for yeast to act, although you must allow time for the dough to rest and (in the case of ribbon pasta) to dry, and for rolling out. However, this is time well spent, since few dishes will give such genuine gastronomic pleasure as fresh, delicate tagliatelle or cannelloni. You may only be able to produce them on occasions, but for a dinner-party or a weekend lunch or supper they are ideal.

• Making Pasta By Hand •

To make pasta, all you have to do is knead and roll out a dough of eggs and flour, with or without the addition of semolina, and either cut it into strips or, for stuffed pasta, add the filling (see pages 100–19) and cut it into squares (or circles). However, rolling it out will need a little practice. With the recipes I have given below, you will be able to make good pasta the first time you try (this has been proved by the testing-team) and it will improve with subsequent attempts. You will also find that it becomes quicker; nevertheless, even when you are skilled you will still need to allow over an hour for the whole operation of pasta-making, because the dough has to be left for at least 25–30 minutes after kneading before you roll it out. But you can leave it for several hours and roll it out later, whenever is convenient, provided you cover it to prevent it from drying out.

• EQUIPMENT •

You will need a space about 50 cm/20 inches square for rolling-out and, if you are making ribbon pasta, something on which to hang the dough to dry. For rolling, a pastry-board will be too small: a smooth melamine or well-scrubbed wooden table-top serves admirably. (I use a piece of melamine-coated chipboard sold for shelving, which cost £1.80p.) For hanging out the dough, I suggest a broom or broom-handle propped across two chairs (broom-handles cost about 80p); failing this, use the chair-backs.

The only other pieces of equipment you need are a fairly heavy, sharp knife and a rolling-pin. A rolling-pin is essential: if necessary, you can use an ordinary pastry-pin, but a longer one will make rolling out both easier and quicker, partly because pastry-pins are too short to roll the whole width of the dough at once. Long, Italian-style pins can be bought at good kitchen-shops and departments, or from catering suppliers. Traditional wooden ones (from kitchen shops and departments only) cost £2.50p–£3.00; newer, more hygenic nylon ones (from catering suppliers) £11–£15.50p, which is dear but represents a long-term investment.

• STORAGE AND HYGIENE •

As I have said in the Introduction, ribbon pasta can be kept fresh for two days: wrap in foodwrap and store in the refrigerator. Alternatively, it can be dried and kept for 3–4 weeks at room temperature: store in a large tin or box (an empty cereal packet is ideal). Line the container with rice- or greaseproof paper; do not wrap in foodwrap, as the complete exclusion of air will encourage mould. Lasagne and cannelloni (see pages 120 and 109) can be made, partly or entirely, a day ahead;

ravioli stuffed with spinach (see page 105) can also be made a day in advance, and kept in the refrigerator.

In the interests of both health and flavour, use the freshest possible free-range eggs. Also for reasons of health, wash your hands before and after handling the dough and the rolling-surface and all utensils directly after use.

• MEASUREMENTS •

I have given metric measurements first in the recipes. When measuring flour, it is preferable to follow the more accurate metric measurements to give the best results.

• THE RECIPES •

Below are two sets of recipes: the first is based on a rich dough made with two whole eggs and two yolks, which I suggest you try to begin with. The standard recipe calls for four whole eggs, which is more economical but gives a dough which is a little fragile and sometimes breaks; the resulting pasta can also be tough. With only two egg-whites (and less flour) the dough is easier to handle, will not tear, and infallibly makes good pasta. I would choose this recipe in any case for making stuffed pasta, especially ravioli. This will make enough for 3–4 people or about 410 g/14 oz.

For the second set, four whole eggs are used and (in most cases) a proportion of semolina, which prevents the dough from tearing and ensures that the pasta will have good texture: as the semolina makes the dough slightly harder to roll, I have also added a little oil. I recommend this recipe for tagliatelle and other ribbon pasta when you want to make enough for 4–6.

• RICH EGG PASTA •

For this, I have given a number of variations: brown and wholemeal pasta; with a proportion of maize flour; or tomato-, spinach-, garlic and herb-, or chilli-flavoured. The flavoured pastas give only background taste; however, the garlic and herb smells very good and the tomato looks most attractive. The spinach, unfortunately, does not come out so green as when it is machine-rolled (it is also the only recipe with which anyone has had problems).

Since it is difficult to judge the thickness of the sheets of dough as you roll, until you have had experience, I have supplied measurements: these are, however, merely guides (the sheets in any case will not be symmetrical).

The amounts of flour specified can also only be guides. Flours vary in absorbency; despite grading, eggs differ slightly in size; in addition, where egg-yolks as well as whole eggs are needed, the exact quantity of flour will depend on how completely you separate the eggs. A little extra egg-white in the dough does not matter, but will mean that a little extra flour is absorbed. If you find that you do not have enough, add more; if there is too much, leave the surplus in the bottom of the bowl. *For* 3–4.

• INGREDIENTS •

½ teaspoonful salt

250 *g/9 oz plain white flour*

2 *size-2 egg-yolks*

2 *size-2 free-range eggs*

Plain white flour for dusting

Rolling-pin, 50 cm/20 inches long, if possible
Scales
Largish mixing bowl
Teaspoon
Rolling-out surface at least 50 cm/20 inches square
Fairly heavy, sharp knife

FOR RIBBON PASTA

Kitchen paper or 2 clean tea-towels
Broom-handle, broom, or 2 chair-backs

• METHOD •

1 Mix the salt with the flour in the bowl. Make a well in the

middle. Take two eggs: wash them (in case bits of shell fall into them), crack each sharply in the middle, and break over a saucer or small bowl, holding it at an angle, so that the yolk does not escape. Tip the yolk from one half shell to the other until all the white has fallen out. Empty the yolks into the well. If you are making ribbon pasta, keep the whites for something else (see page 187). Add the remaining two eggs to the yolks.
2 Wash and dry your hands. Combine the flour with the egg gradually, using your fingers (or a spoon if you prefer); start from the centre of the bowl and work outwards until an apparently stiffish dough is formed. All the flour will not be taken up: do not try to mix it in but leave it at the bottom of the bowl. Wash your hands again. Divide the dough into four small balls and knead each in turn. Hold the dough in the palm of one hand and dig your thumb and the backs of your fingers into it until it is smooth, glossy, and elastic. By the time it is kneaded sufficiently, you should be able to pull it out, Chinese-style, into quite a long strip without it breaking. For all four balls, this will take a good 10 minutes. As you knead, the dough will become sticky: roll it in flour and work the flour into it until no patches of stickiness remain. Do not, however, add so much that it becomes difficult to knead, since this will also make it hard to roll.

Sprinkle a very little flour over the kneaded balls, cover with foodwrap, and leave to rest for a minimum of 25 minutes.
3 Prepare the rolling-out surface. For ribbon pasta, set the broom-handle across two chairs; cover with kitchen paper or one of the tea-towels. Very lightly dust the rolling-surface and -pin with flour. Re-knead the first portion of dough briefly and form it into a round ball. Roll it into a circle the size of a large plate, turning it slightly between each roll to ensure that it remains round. If you have a long pin, you can now use a method of rolling which I tried after reading *The Classic Italian Cookbook* by Marcella Hazan (Papermac, 1973) and found transformed rolling into a rapid, effortless process. Curl the side of the dough furthest away from you round the pin and roll towards you, using a gentle but firm backwards-and-forwards motion, until all the dough is rolled up. As you roll, stretch the dough on the pin towards the ends with your hands. Then roll it out flat, still using a to-and-fro motion. If any of it sticks to itself, ease it

apart and sprinkle with a little flour. The result of the to-and-fro rolling is dramatic: you will find that the circle has become elliptical. Roll out any puckers, turn it to 90 degrees so that you are curling the long side over the pin, and repeat. Unless you are making lasagne, continue until the sheet is transparent and roughly 36 cm/14 inches in diameter: this will probably take 4–5 minutes. For ribbon pasta, hang the sheet to dry on the broom-handle: for stuffed pasta, turn to pages 100–19.

If you have only a pastry rolling-pin, you may not be able to use the method described above; to-and-fro double rolling, however, is still very helpful. Roll away from you; do not be too vigorous, since repetition is more effective than pressure. Turn the sheets after each roll, adding a slight sprinkling of flour if necessary.

Do not interrupt rolling, since once it has been stretched, the dough will quickly lose its elasticity. Frayed edges do not matter; similarly, if by any chance you accidentally catch the dough or roll unevenly so that a hole appears, leave it: the pasta can be cut round it but cannot be re-rolled without considerable difficulty.

4 For stuffed pasta or lasagne, see pages 100–17 and 120–2 respectively. For ribbon pasta, repeat with a second and third lump: if rolling has been slow, check to see whether the first is dry enough to cut before rolling out the fourth. Drying takes about 15 minutes: the sheet should be slightly paper-like but still perfectly pliable. Lay kitchen paper or the remaining tea-towel over a space on the work-surface or a table. Place the sheet to be cut on a board or the rolling-out surface (but bear in mind that cutting could score it) and trim into an oblong with the knife. Fold about 2.5 cm/1 inch from the top and bottom edges towards the centre. Continue to fold towards the centre until the two rolls meet. Level the ends and cut across the rolls into strips. Tagliatelle should be about 5 mm/¼ inch wide; tagliarini/tagliolini 2 mm/$^{1}/_{10}$ inch wide. Hang the folded strips over your hand: each side will then fall out straight. (The chef and cookery writer Clara Tomasi showed me this way of folding, which saves time, for if you roll up the sheet like a Swiss roll, each strip will have to be straightened by hand.) Spread out the cut strips on the tea-towel or kitchen paper to dry further. Repeat with the other sheets of dough. As far as possible, keep the strips separate; if you run out of space, place the newest on top of those you cut first. To keep as fresh pasta, leave for about 20 minutes: the strands must be dry enough not to stick together but still soft. Wrap in foodwrap and store in the refrigerator. To dry completely, leave in a warm place for 4–5 hours, until brittle: store in a tin or packet lined with greaseproof paper.

• Brown Pasta •

Fresh wholemeal pasta will almost certainly have to be made at home because at present (at the time of going to press) it is virtually impossible to buy it. Brown or a mixture of brown and white flour, however, makes excellent pasta: in my view, its only disadvantage is that it does not go well with cheese – although, having said this, I have often served it with Parsley Pesto (see page 65), which contains pecorino cheese but suits the pasta because it has a crunchy texture and the predominant flavour is garlic.

As 100% wholemeal is hard to knead and roll, I am giving a recipe for half wholemeal, half white flour first, which tastes positively of the brown flour but is lighter-textured and easier to handle. *For 3–4.*

• INGREDIENTS •

125 g/4½ oz finely ground plain wholemeal flour

125 g/4½ oz plain white flour

½ teaspoonful salt

2 size-2 egg-yolks

2 size-2 free-range eggs

Plain white flour for dusting

Equipment as for Rich Egg Pasta, page 19

• METHOD •

Thoroughly mix the flours and salt and proceed as above. You may find, however, that the sheets dry more quickly: check the first and cut it if necessary after rolling the second.

• WHOLEMEAL PASTA •

This dough is stiffer than in the previous recipes and will not pull out into a string. Allow a little extra time for rolling. *For* 3–4.

• INGREDIENTS •

225 g/8 oz finely ground plain wholemeal flour

1/2 teaspoonful salt

2 size-2 egg-yolks

2 size-2 eggs

Plain wholemeal flour for dusting

Equipment as for Rich Egg Pasta, page 19

• METHOD •

Proceed as for Rich Egg Pasta. The sheets will roll out slightly smaller: aim for 32–33 cm/13 inches diameter. Also, as with Brown Pasta, they may dry quickly: check and if necessary cut the first after rolling out the second.

• MAIZE PASTA •

A proportion of maize flour makes exceptionally delicate, melting (rather than soft) pasta; the taste of the maize comes across surprisingly strongly.

It is essential to use finely ground maize flour (available from health-food shops) rather than coarser polenta meal. *For* 3–4.

• INGREDIENTS •

90 g/3 1/2 oz maize flour

180 g/scant 6 oz plain white flour

3/4 teaspoonful salt

2 size-2 egg-yolks

2 size-2 free-range eggs

Plain white flour for dusting

Equipment as for Rich Egg Pasta, page 19

• METHOD •

Follow the directions for Rich Egg Pasta. The dough is very absorbent and easy to knead, but slightly fragile: take care not to tear it when rolling.

• TOMATO PASTA •

According to whether you add 1 or 2 tablespoonsful of tomato purée, this will be either rosy melon yellow or deep orange. Less purée will give a better texture but the orange looks more dramatic. As the purée absorbs flour, you will make more pasta than with the preceding recipes: certainly with 2 tablespoonsful there should be *plenty for* 4.

• INGREDIENTS •

½ teaspoonful salt

290 g/10½ oz or 330 g/11½ oz plain white flour

2 size-2 egg-yolks

2 size-2 eggs

1 or 2 tablespoonsful tomato purée (2 with 330 g/11½ oz flour)

Plain white flour for dusting

Equipment as for Rich Egg Pasta, page 19

• METHOD •

Mix the salt with the flour; make a well in the middle of the flour. Separate and add the eggs as before. Add the tomato purée and continue as for Rich Egg Pasta. You should be able to roll the sheets of dough to a diameter of about 38 cm/15 inches or 40 cm/16 inches.

• CHILLI PASTA •

This pasta is a warm pink.

Use exactly the same ingredients as for Rich Egg Pasta but with the addition of 3 teaspoonsful hot chilli powder. Mix the chilli powder with the flour and salt and proceed exactly as before. *For* 3–4.

• GARLIC AND HERB PASTA •

The raw dough is pale green with darker flecks; most of the colour, however, is lost during cooking.

The moisture in the flavourings means that, as with Tomato Pasta, more flour is absorbed than with Rich Egg Pasta. *For* 3–4.

• INGREDIENTS •

2 fat sprigs parsley	*½ teaspoonful salt*
3 cloves garlic	*2 size-2 egg-yolks*
2 teaspoonsful dried oregano	*2 size-2 free-range eggs*
275 g/10 oz plain white flour	*Plain white flour for dusting*

Equipment as for Rich Egg Pasta, page 19

• METHOD •

1 Wash the parsley, blot completely dry, and chop finely. Peel and roughly chop the garlic. Crush the garlic in a mortar; add and thoroughly pound the parsley. Stir in the oregano.

2 Mix the flour and salt and make a well in the middle. Separate the egg-yolks and add, plus the eggs, as before. Add the garlic and herbs and continue as for Rich Egg Pasta. You may need to dust the sheets frequently with flour while rolling. Roll to a diameter of about 38 cm/15 inches.

• Spinach Pasta •

The moisture in the spinach, which seeps out gradually during kneading and rolling, means that extra flour will probably be needed at all stages. If the dough remains too moist after rolling and drying, the pasta will be soggy. At the risk of seeming very extravagant, I suggest using three rather than two egg-yolks to improve texture. I also advise against trying this recipe until you have gained a little experience.

Sometimes a vegetable which looks similar to spinach, but has larger leaves and thick, white stems, is sold instead: this is beet spinach or sea-kale beet. For some purposes this is an acceptable substitute, but it will give a disappointing result here, since it will not colour the pasta as effectively as real spinach. With proper spinach, the pasta will be a pleasant but not vivid green with dark flecks. *For* 3–4.

• INGREDIENTS •

250 g/9 oz spinach

275 g/10 oz plain white flour

Salt

3 size-2 egg-yolks

1 size-2 free-range egg

Plain white flour for dusting

Equipment as for Rich Egg Pasta, page 19
Saucepan with a lid
Sieve

• METHOD •

1 Pick over the spinach, removing any roots, weeds, or damaged leaves. Wash, twice if necessary, and put into the saucepan with 1/4 teaspoonful salt and 1 tablespoonful water. Put on the lid, set over medium heat, and cook for 4 minutes. Stir and continue to cook, covered, 1–2 minutes, until the spinach is submerged in liquid and just tender. Drain and press out as much moisture as possible with the back of a spoon. Chop finely.

2 Mix the flour with 1/2 a teaspoonful salt; make a well in the middle. Separate the eggs as before and empty into the well. Add the whole egg and the spinach. Continue as for Rich Egg Pasta but knead for a minute or two extra to ensure that no pockets of unmixed spinach remain in the dough before rolling. Dust with flour between each rolling. Dry the sheets for 20, and the cut strips for 30, minutes.

• Semolina and Egg Pasta •

This is a slightly harder kind of pasta than Rich Egg but still has excellent texture. It kneads and rolls easily but takes a little longer to make because you are handling more dough. *For 4–6.*

• INGREDIENTS •

340 g/12 oz plain white flour
150 g/5 oz fine semolina
1 level teaspoonful salt
4 size-2 free-range eggs
1 tablespoonful olive oil
Plain white flour for sprinkling

Equipment as for Rich Egg Pasta, page 19

• METHOD •

Thoroughly mix the flour, semolina, and salt. Make a well in the middle, add the eggs and the oil, and proceed as for Rich Egg Pasta. Roll the sheets to a diameter of 43–45 cm/17–18 inches.

• Brown Semolina Pasta •

This recipe will make enough *for 4–6.*

• INGREDIENTS •

200 g/7 oz finely ground plain wholemeal flour
1 level teaspoonful salt
4 size-2 free-range eggs

125 g/4½ oz plain white flour

125 g/4½ oz fine semolina

1 tablespoonful olive oil

Plain white flour for dusting

Equipment as for Rich Egg Pasta, page 19

• METHOD •

Mix the flours, semolina, and salt together. Make a well in the middle, then add the eggs and oil, and proceed exactly as for Rich Egg Pasta.

• Oil and Wholemeal Pasta •

This is made with whole eggs but by definition does not contain semolina. As with the previous recipe for wholemeal flour, it is relatively stiff to knead and roll. *For* 4–6.

• INGREDIENTS •

440 g/15½ oz finely ground wholemeal flour

1 level teaspoonful salt

4 size-2 free-range eggs

1 tablespoonful olive oil

Fine plain wholemeal flour for dusting

Equipment as for Rich Egg Pasta, page 19

• METHOD •

Mix the flour and salt. Make a well in the middle, add the eggs and oil, and proceed as for Rich Egg Pasta.

• Tomato Semolina Pasta •

This comes out a deep orange colour but has good texture. The moisture in the tomatoe purée means that only 3 eggs are needed. *For* 4.

• INGREDIENTS •

250 g/9 oz plain white flour

175 g/6 oz fine semolina

2/3 teaspoonful salt

3 fairly heaped tablespoonsful tomato purée

3 size-2 free-range eggs

Plain white flour for dusting

Equipment as for Rich Egg Pasta, page 19

• METHOD •

Thoroughly mix the flour, semolina, and salt. Make a well in the middle and add the eggs. Add the purée. Continue as for Rich Egg Pasta.

• Making Pasta with a Machine •

I am including directions for using a pasta-machine, not because I imagine that many readers will have one, but for the sake of completeness. As the standard type of hand-operated machine (which costs £28–30) is extremely simple and easy to use, and (unusually) comes with fairly clear instructions, I need say relatively little. The basic unit, without attachments, rolls the dough and has cutters for tagliatelle and tagliolini/tagliarini, leaving you to mix, knead, and, unless you are making a stuffed pasta dish, dry the dough before and after cutting: you will therefore need a broom-handle, space for laying out the cut strips, and tea-towels or kitchen paper as for hand-made pasta.

To make the pasta, mix and knead any of the recipes given for dough with two eggs and two yolks; leave it to rest for a minimum of 25 minutes, as before. Clear a surface on the edge of a work-top or table about 18 cm/7 inches deep and 50 cm/20 inches long. Wipe the machine with a dry cloth if necessary and clamp it to the side of the table in the middle of the space (the area at each side of it is to receive the dough as it is extruded, so make sure that it is perfectly clean; alternatively, spread it with extra tea-towels or kitchen paper). Slot the handle into the hole on the rolling side and set the rollers to the widest of a series of ratchets. Wash your hands. Re-knead the first ball of dough briefly, form it into a sausage, and feed it through the rollers. It will emerge as a strip. If it is at all sticky, dust one side with flour. Fold it in half with the flour on the inside and feed it through again. Repeat the folding and rolling 8 times. After the eighth, do not fold it: instead, set the rollers to the next, slightly narrower, ratchet. Feed it through, set the rollers to the next ratchet, and repeat up to the narrowest. When the strip becomes very long, cut it. For ribbon pasta, hang it to dry and repeat with the rest of the dough; for stuffed pasta, see pages 100–19. To cut tagliatelle or tagliarini, move the handle to the appropriate cutter, feed in the strips, and lay them out to dry.

The machine can be used with the recipes for semolina and four whole eggs but it is advisable to roll out the dough briefly by hand and fold it before machine-rolling, because the semolina will otherwise cause it to crumble at first. With a machine there is really no need for semolina: for a dough using whole eggs, I recommend the standard recipe given below.

When you have finished using the machine, turn the rollers and cutters briefly to dislodge fragments of dough and wipe it with dry kitchen paper. One of its bonuses is that it cannot be washed up: for this reason, however, it should be kept covered.

• Plain Egg Pasta •

This makes enough ribbon pasta *for* 4–6. To vary the quantity, allow 1/4 teaspoonful salt and about 110 g/4 oz flour per size-2 egg (smaller eggs will absorb less flour).

With 4 whole eggs, divide the dough into 8 rather than 4 lumps before feeding it through the machine.

• INGREDIENTS •

440 *g/15 1/2 oz plain white flour*
1 *level teaspoonful salt*
4 *size-2 free-range eggs*

• METHOD •

Follow the general instructions already given.

• PASTA SOUPS •

All the following recipes are quite substantial enough to serve as a meal, except perhaps Yoghurt Soup (see page 32), which I have suggested accompanying with crudities and *masala puri* (a version of poppadam).

Typically, Chinese-style soups are made on a different principle from that which has evolved in the West: instead of cooking ingredients slowly, with or without stock, to extract flavour, stock is made first and (as with stir-frying) the solid ingredients cooked very quickly so that they retain their crispness and flavour. This method necessitates making stock, which, although it can be very cheap, was unpopular with the testing-team. I have therefore included only one soup of this type (Chicken Noodle, page 40).

A general point to bear in mind when making pasta soups is that pasta is absorbent and will continue to take in liquid after cooking. This means that you should not add it until just before the meal, allowing only enough time for it to become tender. If the soup is left standing, the pasta will become swollen and soggy and the amount of liquid in the soup correspondingly reduced (this applies particularly to Yoghurt Soup, which contains a relatively high proportion of pasta: after a few hours the pasta will be huge and the soup itself will almost have disappeared).

• Yoghurt Soup with • Pasta Shells

Yoghurt soup is a standard Indian dish, but this version of it, with pasta shells, comes from the cookery writer and demonstrator Kumud Shah. The soup is quick and easy, healthy, and remarkably cheap: with the possible exception of chick-pea flour, which can be bought at health-food shops, anyone used to cooking with spices will probably have all the ingredients needed anyway.

It is important, however, to use ordinary whole-milk smooth- or thick-set yoghurt: low-fat will not give a satisfactorily rich, creamy result and may curdle, and natural-set (which is not smooth and homogeneous) will almost certainly curdle. The taste of the yoghurt also matters, since if it is very sharp it will make the soup too sour, while very mild (such as Greek or Greek-style) does not give sufficient background for the spicy flavouring. (If, however, you do use genuine, imported Greek yoghurt, which is very thick, add a little extra water.)

Serve with poppadams or *masala puri* (see page 34), radishes, and/or chopped green pepper. The pepper should be firm and glossy and the radishes hard rather than spongy: if you can find them, choose the tapered, half-red, half-white kind. F*or* 3.

• INGREDIENTS •

3 *cm*/1 1/4 *inch piece root ginger*

6 *cloves*

1 *green chilli*

2.5 *cm*/1 *inch piece cinnamon stick*

1 *teaspoonful mustard seeds*

1 *teaspoonful cumin seeds*

1 *teaspoonful coriander seeds*

25 *g*/1 *oz chick-pea flour*

375 *g*/13 *oz smooth-set whole-milk yoghurt*

2 *tablespoonsful corn or groundnut oil*

1 *teaspoonful salt*

Pinch turmeric (optional)

200 *g*/7 *oz small pasta shells*

FOR SERVING (OPTIONAL)

Bunch radishes

Poppadams or puri

1 *green pepper*

Largish saucepan
Teaspoon
Tablespoon
Pestle and mortar
Bowl
Fork, or egg rotary whisk
Sieve
Kitchen paper
Frying-pan for *puri*

• METHOD •

1 Prepare the spices. Peel and finely chop the ginger, throwing away any fibrous patches. Crush the cloves, wash the chilli, and break the cinnamon into 3 or 4 pieces. Put all four into the saucepan. Crush the mustard seed, cumin, and coriander (but do not put into the saucepan).

2 Place the chick-pea flour in a bowl and stir in the yoghurt. Add 900 ml/1 1/2 pints water. Beat until smooth and well mixed with a fork or egg-whisk (if possible, use a rotary whisk). As the chick-pea flour tends to form lumps, strain through a sieve.

3 Add the oil to the spices in the saucepan and warm over medium/low heat. Add the remaining spices and fry until they start to splutter or are just beginning to be tinged with colour. Pour in the yoghurt mixture and bring just to the boil. Add the salt and turmeric (which is needed only to give the soup a creamy colour), stir, and lower the heat to a simmer. Do not stir again: except for the addition of the pasta, the soup must now be left undisturbed for 15 minutes. Check how long the pasta takes to cook and add it at the appropriate time, pressing it gently into the liquid. When the 15 minutes are up, remove the soup from the heat; let it stand for a moment or two and serve.

4 If you are making *puri*, fry them while the soup simmers and prepare the radishes and pepper beforehand; otherwise, wash and chop the vegetables during this time. Cut off the leaves of the radishes if they have not already been trimmed, leaving short lengths of stem if you like; remove the ends of the roots, wash, and blot dry. Wash, dry, and quarter the pepper; remove the white inner flesh and all the seeds, and cut into strips.

• MASALA PURI •

When Kumud showed me how to make these, she used an Indian rolling-pin, which was made of beautifully grained and polished wood and was much thinner even than a pasta rolling-pin. And instead of using a board, she rolled out the *puri* on an Indian rolling-out stool, which reminded me of a milking-stool.

The dough should be kneaded and rolled before you make the soup; the *puri* can be fried while it simmers. Do not fry them far in advance, since they stay crisp only for a short time.

If possible, fry them in corn oil, which gives a much cleaner, fresher taste than groundnut oil. *Makes 16 teacup-sized rounds.*

• INGREDIENTS •

125 g/4½ oz plain white flour and 125 g/4½ oz finely ground wholemeal flour or 250 g/9 oz plain white flour

1 teaspoonful salt

1 teaspoonful hot chilli powder

½ teaspoonful turmeric

200–250 ml/about ⅜ pint corn oil, plus 1 extra dessertspoonful

5–6 tablespoonsful water

Extra white flour for spinkling

2 or 3 small squares of bread

Bowl
Rolling-pin (any)
Rolling-out surface about 30 cm/12 inches square
Teacup or similar-sized round pastry-cutter
Fish-slice or perforated spoon
Greaseproof or kitchen paper

• METHOD •

1 Mix the flour or flours with the salt and spices. Make a well in the middle. Add 1 dessertspoonful of oil and 5 tablespoonsful of water and form into a dough, adding more water as needed to take up all the flour. Divide into 4 balls, as for pasta dough, and knead for 5 minutes or until smooth, glossy and elastic enough to pull out into a string without breaking.

2 Lightly sprinkle the rolling-pin and surface with flour and roll the first ball of dough into a circle about 25 cm/10 inches in diameter: this is by no means as thin as for pasta and, as the dough is as easy as possible to roll, takes very little time. Cut 4 circles from it with the teacup or pastry-cutter and place on the greaseproof paper. Repeat with the rest of the dough. Do not re-roll the trimmings: although they will roll out easily, the resulting *puri* will be tough.

3 Place a dish or a couple of plates lined with kitchen paper to hand near the cooker. Pour about 2 cm/¾ inch of oil into a smallish saucepan: the smaller the pan, the less oil you will need, but it is essential to use one large enough to cover the ring completely, since hot oil catches fire easily. You should also be careful to place it with the handle at the sides or back, where there is no danger of knocking it, thus causing hot fat to spill. Heat over a moderate to high heat for about 1 minute and lower a cube of bread into it on the fish-slice: if it turns golden in 40–60 seconds, the oil is hot enough for frying the *puri*. (I use the word 'lower' because if you drop items suddenly into hot oil, it may splutter in your face.) Lower the first round of dough into the oil and fry for a few seconds, until it is puffed up and the underside golden. Turn and fry until the other side is golden. Remove and place on a plate lined with kitchen paper. Repeat with the rest of the dough. Eat the *puri* promptly.The oil can be re-used at least once: leave to cool, strain and store in a stoppered bottle.

• Macaroni, Broccoli and • Tomato soup

I once asked the chef Carla Tomasi which was her favourite soup: she replied without hesitation, 'Broccoli and Tomato'. I did not ask her for a recipe and do not know if this is anything like her version, but it is certainly one of *my* favourites. The two flavours go together perfectly, needing no addition of herbs or spices; to develop their full richness, however, really does call for long, slow cooking, as indicated below (total cooking-time is about 80 minutes). You can make the soup up to the addition of pasta several hours in advance (but preferably not the day before, since it loses the edge of its flavour if kept for any length of time). After the addition of the pasta, eat immediately.

The beans need soaking overnight. F*or* 4.

• INGREDIENTS •

100 *g*/3½ *oz butter beans, soaked overnight*

Salt

375 *g*/13 *oz broccoli*

2 *medium sticks celery (not from the outside)*

1 *largish onion* (150–190 *g*/5 *oz*)

4–5 *cloves garlic*

1 *kg*/2 *lb* 4 *oz ripe tomatoes*

3 *tablespoonsful olive oil*

Pepper

3 *tablespoonsful tomato purée*

1 *teaspoonful soft brown sugar*

90 *g*/3½ *oz brown or white macaroni (brown suits the dish but white looks more attractive)*

Wok or large saucepan with a lid
Smaller saucepan with a lid
Tablespoon
Teaspoon
Colander
2 bowls
Kitchen paper

• METHOD •

1 Rinse the beans in cold water and put them into the smaller saucepan with a lid. Add 900 ml/1½ pints cold water (but no salt), bring to the boil, and skim. Boil briskly for 5 minutes. Lower the heat, cover, and simmer 40 minutes; add a small pinch of salt and simmer for another 10–15 minutes or until just tender. Drain over a bowl and keep the cooking-liquor.

2 Chop the broccoli into florets not more than 1.5 cm/2/3 inch long and 1.25 cm/1/2 inch wide at the flower end. Wash and place in a bowl lined with kitchen paper to dry. Trim the leaf and root ends of the celery, pare off any brownish streaks, and wash. Dry with kitchen paper and slice finely. Peel and finely chop the onion and garlic, keeping them separate. Skin and chop the tomatoes, throwing away the hard cores.
3 Put the oil into the wok or large saucepan with a lid and fry the onion and celery over very low heat, stirring occasionally, for 5 minutes. Add the garlic and broccoli, season generously with salt, cover, and continue to cook over very low heat, stirring constantly, for 10–15 minutes or until the onion is just starting to change colour (the broccoli may also begin to turn a little brown: this does not matter). Add the tomato, season with a little salt and rather more pepper, cover, and simmer 30–35 minutes, stirring often; if necessary, add a little water. By this time most of the tomato will have liquefied and the broccoli will be very soft. Press any remaining lumps of tomato and the broccoli against the bottom of the pan until the tomato is smooth and the broccoli has disintegrated: it should look rather like finely chopped herbs. Stir in the sugar and tomato purée. Make up the bean liquor to its original 900 ml/1 1/2 pints with water, and add. Stir, cover, and simmer 15 minutes. Add the beans and macaroni and boil gently for as long as the macaroni takes to cook.

Serve with crusty bread.

• SEAFOOD SOUP •

Given the prices of fish and shellfish, no kind of seafood soup is going to be very cheap (except perhaps mussel soup, but in this the cheapness of mussels is offset by the fact that they really do need to be cooked with white wine). The following, however, is one of the most popular I have devised and very reasonable in cost. The bacon and smoked cod ensure that it has plenty of flavour; you may think that you do not like calamari (squid) because of its rubbery texture, but if you choose small or medium-sized fish, which will give you a whole one, or better still two for the weight, and take care not to overcook it, you will find that it is delicate and tender. I have used it here to give the soup body and to match the texture of the pasta. (Do not be dismayed by the dark 'ink' with which it may be surrounded.) You will probably not be able to buy it at your local supermarket, but it will be stocked by any good fishmonger.

If possible, choose fresh (i.e. chilled) and ideally unshelled prawns rather than frozen, since they will be juicier and have much more flavour; if, however, you do use frozen ones, remember that they will take several hours to defrost.

The soup does not involve stock, is easy to make, and fairly quick to cook (cooking-time is about 45 minutes).

Serve with crusty bread. *For* 4.

• INGREDIENTS •

750 g/1 lb 8 oz ripe tomatoes

1 medium onion

3 cloves garlic

Small bunch parsley (enough for 1 heaped tablespoonful when chopped)

1 green chilli

125 g/4½ oz bacon

125 g/4½ oz shelled or 250 g/9 oz unshelled prawns

250 g/9 oz smoked cod

250 g/9 oz calamari

1 tablespoonful olive oil

Salt

Pepper

1 tablespoonful tomato purée

125 g/4½ oz brown or white small pasta shells or thin-cut macaroni

Sharp knife
Kitchen paper
3 plates
Scissors
Saucepan

• METHOD •

1 Skin and chop the tomatoes, throwing away the hard cores. Peel and finely chop the onion and garlic; keep each separate. Trim the stems and wash the parsley, blot dry with kitchen paper, and chop finely. Wash and dry the chilli, remove the

stalk end and seeds, and dice as finely as possible. Do not rub your eyes while handling it and wash your hands afterwards.
2 Trim the rind from the bacon and cut into small strips (use scissors to do this).
3 Shell the prawns if necessary: remove the heads, pull the shell from the tails and pick off any remaining bits of shell over the body. Rinse briskly under the cold tap. Rinse fresh shelled ones; drain frozen ones.
4 Skin the cod: pull the skin sharply from the thickest corner. If it does not come away cleanly, ease it off with a knife. Rinse the flesh under the cold tap and chop into small squares (the size is not important, since it will flake when cooked anyway).
5 Clean the calamari. Pull off the head(s): the innards, including the sac which contains the ink, will come away with it. Discard both (in fact, the ink and tentacles are edible, but I do not suggest using them here). Pull out the flat, transparent central bone or 'pen'. If the fish has not been skinned, peel off the dark skin. Wash the body in cold water, remove any remaining bits of skin, and cut off the fins. Now turn the body inside out like a sock, folding the flesh at the head end back over the outside. The initial folding back may need firmness, but thereafter turning is easy. Thoroughly wash the inside, removing any slimy filaments. Cut the body into fine rings and the fins into strips.
6 Fry the onion and bacon in the oil over low heat, turning often, for 5 minutes; add the garlic and fry for another 8–10 minutes or until the onion is soft and the bacon fat becoming translucent. Add the tomato, season lightly with salt and moderately with pepper, and simmer for 15–20 minutes, pressing the flesh against the bottom of the pan until dissolved. Stir in the tomato purée. Add 900 ml/1 1/2 pints water and bring just to the boil. Check on the packet how long the pasta takes to cook: if it needs 12 minutes or more, add it before the cod. Add the cod, and cook at just above simmering point for 8 minutes. Add the calamari and cook for 2 minutes; add the prawns and cook for 1 minute more. Remove from the heat, sprinkle with the parsley, and serve immediately.

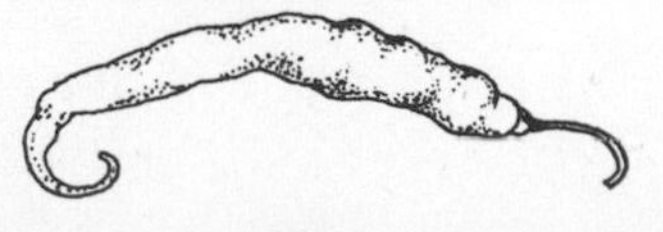

• Chicken Noodle Soup •

This is delicate and fresh-tasting and brings out the flavour of the chicken better than almost any other way of cooking chicken that I know.

There are several advantages of using chicken legs rather than the more usual breasts. Firstly, they are cheaper; secondly, they have more flavour; thirdly, you can make stock from the bones, which you cannot do satisfactorily from breast portions because the bones are too small. (I know how much everyone dislikes the idea of making stock, but, as I have explained in the introduction to this chapter, with Chinese-style soups it is in effect the soup.)

However, leg portions are much more difficult than breasts to cut up, which makes me hesitate to recommend them unreservedly. If you use the breasts instead, you will also need chicken stock-cubes: in this case, omit Step 1 and make up the 2¼ pints of stock according to the instructions on the packet; take care that it is full strength. Put it into (or make it in) the largish saucepan, then proceed with Step 2 as directed below, but omit the salt and simmer the stock for only 25 minutes.

For health reasons, it is particularly important that the chicken should be really fresh: cook it before the sell-by date and bear in mind that you may want to make the stock a day in advance, which will mean keeping the uncooked meat for an extra day.

Choose firm, fresh button mushrooms and if possible smoked ham; avoid sweet-cured.

Oyster sauce is cheap (it costs considerably less than soy) and can be bought at delicatessens or any Chinese store. Particularly if you use chicken breasts and stock-cubes, it is essential to the flavour of the soup. *For* 4.

• INGREDIENTS •

2 free-range chicken legs, weighing about 500–700 *g*/1 *lb* 4 *oz*–1 *lb* 8 *oz*

2 tablespoonsful groundnut oil

2 × 1.5 cm/½ inch pieces root ginger

125 g/4½ oz small button mushrooms

1 outside stick celery

3 or 4 peppercorns

Salt

2 teaspoonsful cornflour

2 tablespoonsful light soy sauce

Pepper

50 g/2 oz lean smoked ham

3 inside sticks celery

250 g/9 oz broccoli

4 or 5 spring onions

250 g/9 oz fine or thread noodles

2 teaspoonsful oyster sauce

Pestle and mortar
Sieve
Bowl
Largish saucepan with a lid
Wok or large saucepan
Sharp knife
Chopping surface, preferably a board, but otherwise a large plate
Teaspoon
Tablespoon
Plate

• METHOD •

1 Prepare the leg bones for stock. To skin chicken legs, pull the skin firmly back over the legs from the thigh end. You may be able to peel it off over the foot, but if not, cut it. Rinse under the cold tap. Bend the leg and cut through the joint to separate thigh and drumstick. Cut the meat from round the bones as closely as possible. Put the bones into a lidded saucepan, and the meat on a plate; if you are making the stock in advance, cover the meat with foodwrap and place at once in the refrigerator. Wash your hands.

2 Peel and slightly crush one piece of ginger with a pestle to release the flavour. Add it to the saucepan. Pull off all or some of the mushroom stalks, trim the bottoms, and wash (set the caps aside: they will be needed later). Add to the saucepan. Trim the leaf end from the outside stick of celery, wash, and slice fairly finely. Add to the saucepan with the peppercorns, a generous pinch of salt, 1 tablespoon of the oil and 1.7 litres/ $2^3/_4$ pints water. Bring to the boil, lower the heat, cover, and simmer $3^1/_2$–4 hours. Strain through a sieve; throw away the bones and vegetables. If the stock has been made in advance, allow to cool, cover, and store in the refrigerator.

3 Dice the meat. Spread out as flat as possible on a chopping surface and cut into pieces about 8 mm/$^1/_4$ inch thick and 2 cm/$^3/_4$ inch long. Cut 2 cm strips across the grain and divide into strips along it, i.e. in the same direction as the bone was placed (you can cut up breasts in either direction, i.e. along or across the grain). Discard any white sinew which you cannot cut. It does not matter if the pieces are irregular in shape, but they should be of about the specified size. Put them into a bowl; wash your hands.

4 Mix the cornflour with 1 tablespoonful soy sauce. Add the second tablespoonful oil and 1 tablespoonful water, season fairly generously with salt and pepper, stir thoroughly, and pour over the chicken. Leave to marinate.

5 Dice the ham. Wash and finely slice the mushroom caps; put with the ham. Trim the leaf and root ends of the celery; pare off any brown streaks, wash, and slice very finely. Cut the broccoli into florets about 2 cm long and not more than 1.5 cm/$^1/_2$ inch wide at the flower ends; wash and add to the celery. Trim the green leaves and the ends of the roots from the onions; peel, sliding off the slippery inner skin, and slice finely. Separate the slices from the white lower ends and the green upper ends (the green slices are for garnishing). Peel and finely slice the second piece of ginger.

6 Set the water to boil for the noodles; start making the soup 5 minutes before the noodles will be ready. Bring the stock to the boil, lower the heat to a fast simmer, i.e. so that it is just bubbling, and add the sliced ginger, ham, and mushrooms. Allow to return to a simmer and cook for 2 minutes. Add the celery, broccoli, and chicken with its marinade. Allow to return to a simmer again and cook for $2^1/_2$ minutes. Add the white onion rings and simmer for 30 seconds. Leave to simmer while you drain the noodles; then remove from the heat. Divide the noodles into serving bowls. Pour the soup over them, leaving some for second helpings. Decorate with the green onion rings and serve.

• Bean and Macaroni Soup •

This is a version (of which there are many) of minestrone. It has virtually every advantage: it is cheap, easy to make, and, although the flavour is considerably enhanced by fresh chicken stock (see page 40), it by no means depends on it. Its character comes partly from the addition of crushed garlic and parsley at the end.

The beans need soaking overnight.

Serve with grated Parmesan or pecorino cheese and hot, crusty bread. *For 4.*

• INGREDIENTS •

50 g/2 oz lean smoked bacon

1 medium onion

500 g/1 lb 2 oz ripe tomatoes

1 medium carrot

2 large or 3 smaller sticks celery

2 tablespoonsful olive oil

1 heaped teaspoonful dried oregano

Pepper

3 pints chicken stock, water, or a mixture

185 g/6 oz haricot beans, soaked overnight

Bunch parsley (enough for 2 heaped tablespoonsful when chopped)

1 large or 2 small cloves garlic

25 g/1 oz pecorino or Parmesan *cheese*

Salt

90 g/3½ oz thin-cut macaroni

Large saucepan or wok with a lid
Tablespoon
Sharp knife
Teaspoon
Bowl
Kitchen paper
Pestle and mortar
Grater (optional)

• METHOD •

1 Trim the rind and any excess fat from the bacon and cut it into strips about 8 mm/¼ inch wide and 1.5 cm/⅔ inch long. Peel and finely chop the onion. Skin and chop the tomatoes, discarding the hard cores. Peel and finely slice the carrot. Trim the leaf and root ends of the celery; wash, pare off any brownish streaks, and slice finely, or dice if the sticks are very large.

2 Fry the onions, bacon, and celery in 1 tablespoonful of the oil over very low heat, turning often, for 5 minutes. Add the carrot and fry for 8–10 minutes; add the oregano and fry for 5 minutes more or until the onion is soft but not brown. Add the tomato, season moderately with pepper (but no salt), and simmer, pressing the lumps of flesh against the bottom of the pan, for 7–10 minutes or until liquefied. Pour in the stock or water. Rinse the beans under the cold tap and add. Raise the heat, bring to the boil, and boil briskly for 5 minutes; then reduce the heat to a simmer, cover, and cook 45 minutes or until the beans are tender.

3 While the soup simmers, trim the stems, wash and blot the parsley dry with kitchen paper. Peel and roughly chop the garlic. Put it into a mortar and pound to a paste. Add and crush the parsley. Finely grate the cheese if necessary; stir it in with the remaining tablespoonful of oil.

4 When the beans are cooked, check to ensure that there is still plenty of liquid in the pan: if necessary, pour in a little more water. Add a moderate pinch of salt and the macaroni and boil gently for the length of time given on the packet or until just tender.

5 Serve the soup with a spoonful of the garlic and parsley mixture on top of each bowl.

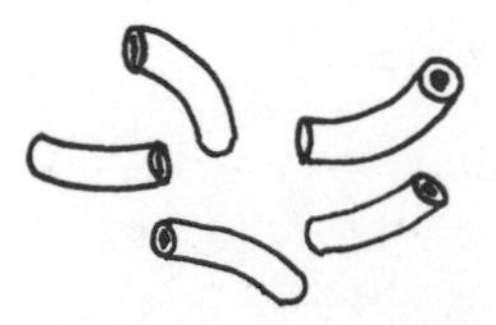

• MICHAEL'S LENTIL SOUP •

I have called the soup Michael's because my husband does not normally like lentils – but he liked this, and was quite sad the next day when he found that a portion that had been left had been entirely absorbed by the macaroni. (Be warned: do not keep the soup after the addition of the pasta.)

It is important to the flavour of the soup to use smoked bacon; partly for the same reason, choose lean streaky rather than back. Streaky is also much cheaper: at the time of going to press, the amount needed (250 g/9 oz) costs only about 90p.

Fresh rosemary is not essential, but if you can manage to obtain it, it rounds off the soup perfectly: you may not actually be able to buy it, but if you know someone with a bush in their garden, they will probably give you a piece (you only need a sprig).

Up to the addition of macaroni, the soup can be made a day in advance. *For* 4–5.

• INGREDIENTS •

250 g/9 oz lean smoked streaky bacon

200 g/7 oz (1 largish) onion

3 large sticks celery (not from the outside)

125 g/4½ oz (1 medium or 2 small) carrots

3 cloves garlic

Sprig fresh rosemary

375 g/13 oz ripe tomatoes

Chicken stock-cube

190 g/6½ oz brown lentils

Salt

1 tablespoonful olive oil

Pepper

2 tablespoonsful tomato purée

125 g/4½ oz thin-cut macaroni or ditali

Saucepan with a lid
Measuring jug
Tablespoon
Sharp knife

Scissors
Kitchen paper
Bowl
Sieve

• METHOD •

1 Remove the rind and any bones from the bacon and cut into strips about 1 cm/½ inch wide and 2 cm/¾ inch long (use kitchen scissors to do this). Peel and finely chop the onion. Trim the leaf and root ends from the celery and pare off any brownish streaks. Wash, dry with kitchen paper, and slice finely. Peel and finely slice the carrot(s) and garlic; wash the rosemary. Skin and chop the tomatoes, throwing away the hard cores. Dissolve the stock-cube in 450 ml/¾ pint boiling water.

2 Rinse the lentils in cold water and put into the saucepan with a lid. Add 1.2 litres/2 pints water (but no salt), bring to the boil, and boil vigorously for 2 minutes. Reduce the heat to a simmer, cover, and cook 30 minutes. Add a little salt and continue to simmer for 5–15 minutes or until soft. Leave until needed in the saucepan.

3 Make sure that the pieces of bacon are not stuck together. Fry with the onion in the oil over very low heat for 5 minutes, turning occasionally. Add the celery, carrot, and garlic and continue to fry very slowly, turning from time to time, for 8–10 minutes. Add the rosemary and fry, turning often, for another 5–10 minutes or until the celery is just soft and the bacon fat and onion translucent but not quite changing colour. Add the tomato, season generously with salt and pepper, and simmer, gently pressing the flesh against the bottom of the pan, for 7–10 minutes or until dissolved. Stir in the tomato purée and add the stock. Simmer 10 minutes.

4 Pour the lentils and lentil liquor into the pan through a sieve; spoon about two-thirds of the lentils into the soup. Press enough of the rest through the sieve to give about 2 tablespoonsful of purée: this will thicken the soup. The remaining contents of the sieve will be fairly thoroughly mashed: add to the soup as they are. Simmer for 10–15 minutes. If you are making the soup the day before, leave to cool, cover, and store in the refrigerator.

5 If the soup was made in advance, stir and heat it slowly:

bring just to the boil. Add the pasta and cook at slightly above simmering point for 7–8 minutes or for as long as it takes to cook. If necessary, add a little extra water. Serve immediately.

• PASTA WITH SAUCES •

• BOILING PASTA •

Three points in particular will make an enormous difference to boiled pasta. The first is to cook it in plenty of water. The amount generally recommended is 1 litre/1¾ pints per 100 g/3½ oz pasta, which means 4 litres/7 pints if you are cooking for 4 people. This calls for a larger saucepan than perhaps you have; however, use the largest possible. If the pasta is boiled in too little water, it will taste murky and stale rather than fresh and clean.

The second point is that the water must be kept boiling. Bring it to a vigorous boil before putting in the pasta, and bring it back to the boil as quickly as possible afterwards (the addition of the cold pasta will reduce its temperature briefly). If the pan has a lid, put it on just until the water re-boils; then remove it, as the pasta should be cooked uncovered. Keep the water at an active, 'rolling' boil for the duration of the cooking.

If you wish, add a few drops of oil to prevent the pasta from sticking together, although with enough water this is not really necessary. Salt the water with one teaspoonful of salt per litre: do not add it to the cold water, but just before putting in the pasta. Add the pasta all at once so that it cooks for the same length of time. Curl long strands of spaghetti round the pan as they soften, and press down any ends that stick up out of the water as promptly as possible. Stir when the water has returned to the boil and at intervals thereafter. (Oriental cooks are always very particular about separating noodles with a fork or chopsticks as they boil.)

The third and most important point about boiling pasta, however, is to cook it for the right length of time. How long this takes cannot be answered in general terms, since different types and – because of differences in flour and manufacture – different brands (even of the same type) take different times. British-packed products carry cooking-times on the packet, which often give a couple of minutes' margin: for serving hot, I recommend the shortest time. Italian brands may not give cooking instructions at all; fresh egg pasta varies according to several factors. A table of average times is given on pages 50–1 to help in co-ordinating the pasta with its accompaniments, but the only reliable way to catch it at the right moment is to test it. Fish out a strand, dip it into cold water and bite it, or try to cut it with a blunt knife. Dried pasta will have reached the *al dente* stage, which is when it is just cooked but still has 'bite' and body, as soon as it is no longer hard in the middle; fresh pasta should be tender and have lost the taste of uncooked flour but still be firm. Pasta that you have made yourself will take longer than the times given, if you rolled the sheets to less than the sizes specified. Wholewheat flour takes a little longer to cook than white. Dough with semolina takes slightly longer than that without. Ribbon pasta, which you have dried out completely, needs about one minute more than when it was fresh.

As soon as the pasta is cooked, drain it by shaking thoroughly but swiftly in a colander. Then, according to how you wish to serve it, add cheese and/or sauce, or a very little oil.

• Serving Pasta •

The most important point about serving is that the pasta should reach the table as hot as possible. The next, but subservient, question is presentation. The simplest method is to place it straight into the serving-bowls with the sauce on top.

More graceful, however, is to toss it with the sauce before serving. This is essential with some dishes (e.g. when it is accompanied by sauces made with cheese or where ingredients are simply fried in oil). With others, whether or not the sauce is tossed, it is important to mix the hot pasta with grated cheese, which gives it background flavour and has a surprisingly different effect from adding the cheese later. On the other hand, mixing the sauce with the pasta may look less attractive than a colourful mound of vegetables on top. To counter this, it is often a good idea to compromise by tossing in only about half of the sauce. Tossing also calls for a large, deep dish, which you may not have. The obvious alternative is to toss the pasta in the hot saucepan in which it was boiled, but this has the disadvantage that the sauce tends to collect round the rim at the bottom. In the end, the decision is yours, and except in cases where tossing really is important to the dish, I have therefore simply given the options.

One other point, which is connected with tossing and keeping the pasta hot, is that not only in China but in Italy too, it is usual to serve it in bowls: the high sides help to conserve heat and make tossing individual portions easier, since stray skeins of long pasta will not slither over the edge. As soup or cereal bowls are ideal, this is an easy custom to follow and will certainly add to the enjoyment of your meal.

• Table of Cooking Times for Boiled Pasta •

These times are to be regarded only as a guide.

DRIED PASTA AND NOODLES

Bucatini 8–10 minutes
Conchiglie (shells) 8–10 minutes
Ditali 10 minutes
Egg noodles 6 minutes
Farfalle (butterflies) 9–11 minutes

Fusilli 9–11 minutes
Macaroni (not quick-cooking) 15–20 minutes
Penne 8–11 minutes
Rigatoni 10–12 minutes
Spaghetti 6–11 minutes
Tagliarini/tagliolini 4 minutes
Tagliatelle 4 minutes
Vermicelli 5 minutes

FRESH PASTA

Capricciosa 3 minutes
Ravioli 2–4 minutes
Tagliarini/tagliolini 1½ minutes
Tagliatelle 4 minutes

• SPAGHETTI WITH • FRESH TOMATO SAUCE

In Italy, tomato sauce is invariably made with long, plum-shaped tomatoes which are sweeter and have a thicker, more jam-like consistency than other kinds; unfortunately, they are seldom available here except in tins. Partly because of the flavour, but mainly because of consistency, many Italian chefs and other Italians in this country refuse to use ordinary fresh tomatoes for sauce and rely entirely on the tinned plum variety. I and other writers have already moaned about the tastelessness of most of the tomatoes in the shops: all the same, since their shortcomings can easily be remedied, I am as firmly in favour of using them for sauce as for using fresh produce for any other purpose. With a dose of tomato purée, which both adds pungency and thickens, plus a little sugar, they make a first-class sauce which is well worth serving in its own right, as well as forming the basis of many other sauces and dishes.

It is important, however, that they should be ripe, since if they are hard and unripe they may not run enough juice for a satisfactory sauce. If yours are hard, spread them out on a rack or in a bowl and leave them for a day or two at room temperature (but keep an eye on them to ensure that they do not become rotten or mouldy).

The celery in the following recipe adds both flavour and texture; however, since the large outside sticks are sometimes tough, use an inner stick if possible. Make sure that it is reasonably tender before adding the tomato purée.

Serve with spaghetti, spaghettini, or short pasta and finely grated pecorino or Parmesan cheese. *For* 4.

• INGREDIENTS •

1 stick celery (not from the outside)
1 medium onion
3 cloves garlic
750 g/1 lb 8 oz ripe tomatoes
1 tablespoonful olive oil
Salt
Pepper
1 level teaspoonful soft brown sugar
1 1/2 tablespoonsful tomato purée
500 g/1 lb 2 oz spaghetti

Tablespoon
Teaspoon
Sharp knife
Small saucepan
Frying-pan
Spatula
Large saucepan
Colander

• METHOD •

1 Discard the leaf and root ends of the celery; wash, dry, and slice finely. Peel and finely chop the onion and garlic; keep each separate.

2 Skin and then chop the tomatoes, throwing away the hard cores.

3 Fry the onion and celery in the oil over low heat, turning often, for 5 minutes; add the garlic and fry 8–10 minutes more or until the celery is soft and the onion soft but not brown. Add the tomatoes. Season lightly with salt and moderately with

pepper, add the sugar, and simmer 7–10 minutes, pressing the tomato flesh against the bottom of the pan until liquefied. Stir in the tomato purée and simmer very gently for 25 minutes.
4 Set the water to boil for the pasta (see pages 50–1 for cooking time) while the sauce simmers.
5 When the pasta is cooked, drain it and either toss some of the sauce into it or serve the sauce on top.

• Creamy Tomato Sauce •

Just 50 g/2 oz cream cheese makes Fresh Tomato Sauce astonishingly rich-tasting and creamy. It is almost salmon coloured: black pasta (which is dyed with cuttle-fish ink) can usually only be bought from delicatessens or pasta shops, but if you can find it, it looks very dramatic with the pale sauce on top.

Make Fresh Tomato Sauce as opposite; beat the cheese with a fork and stir it in just before serving.

You may prefer not to add Parmesan or pecorino, but in that case remember that the dish will contain relatively little protein (cream cheese is mainly fat).

• Spaghetti with • Plum Tomato Sauce

The long, plum-shaped tomatoes used for sauces in Italy can sometimes be bought fresh here but not often enough to make suggesting using them worth while: this recipe is therefore based on tinned ones. It is sweeter and has less body and

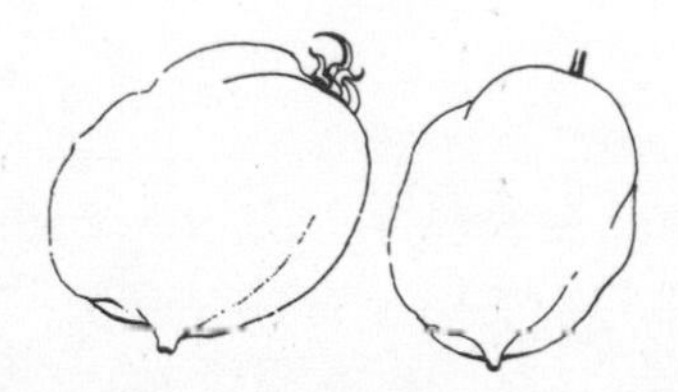

texture than the equivalent made with purée and ordinary tomatoes. Also, one 400 g/14 oz tin yields a smaller quantity than 750 g/1 lb 8 oz fresh tomatoes. But I am sure that I need not add that the tinned tomatoes are cheap and, as they are already skinned, save time.

This recipe can be used instead of Fresh Tomato Sauce to go with Ravioli or Cannelloni Stuffed with Spinach (see page 105) and is particularly suitable for Cannelloni with Mushroom and Mozzarella Stuffing (page 117); tinned rather than fresh tomatoes can also be used for any of the sauces based on tomato in this chapter. Use one tin of tomatoes, only half a teaspoonful of brown sugar, and omit the tomato purée.

Make sure that the celery is reasonably tender before adding the tomatoes.

Serve with spaghetti or spaghettini and finely grated Parmesan or pecorino cheese. *For* 3 *or* 4.

• INGREDIENTS •

1 stick celery (not from the outside)

1 medium onion

3 cloves garlic

1 × 400-g/14-oz tin plain (i.e. unflavoured) peeled plum tomatoes

1 tablespoonful olive oil

Salt

Pepper

½ teaspoonful soft dark brown sugar

375 g/13 oz or 500 g/1 lb 2 oz spaghetti

Tablespoon
Teaspoon
Vegetable knife
Frying-pan
Spatula
Large saucepan
Colander

• METHOD •

1 Discard the leaf and root ends of the celery; wash, dry, and finely slice. Peel and finely chop the onion and garlic. Remove the hard ends and any stray pieces of skin from the tomatoes and chop; keep all the juice.

2 Fry the celery and onion in the oil over low heat, turning often, for 5 minutes. Add the garlic and fry for another 8–10 minutes or until the celery is soft, and the onion soft but not brown. Add the tomatoes with their juice, season moderately with salt and pepper, and add the sugar. Simmer over very low heat, stirring and breaking up the tomato flesh from time to time, for 45–50 minutes or until the sauce is thick.
3 Set the water to boil for the spaghetti (see pages 50–1 for cooking time) while the sauce simmers.
4 When the pasta is cooked, drain it and either toss some of the sauce into it or serve the sauce on top.

• Spaghetti with Aubergine and • Tomato Sauce

This is similar in character to Bacon and Tomato Sauce (see page 79) but if anything even richer-tasting.

Since with both of them cheese is needed as a background flavour, it is better tossed into the pasta as soon as it is cooked than added afterwards; you can serve more separately if you wish.

If you have two pans, fry the aubergine while the sauce is simmering; otherwise, cook it before the sauce. (It is a nuisance to have to cook it separately, but unless it is fried at a higher heat than the other vegetables, it will not be cooked through.)

Allow 1/2–1 hour for it to sweat. For 4.

• INGREDIENTS •

375–500 g/13 oz–1 lb 4 oz aubergine (1 largish)

Fine salt

1 stick celery (not from the outside)

1 medium onion

3 cloves garlic

100 g/3 1/2 oz pecorino cheese

3 1/2 tablespoonsful olive oil

Pepper

1 teaspoonful soft dark brown sugar

1 1/2 tablespoonsful tomato purée

750 g/1 lb 8 oz ripe tomatoes *500 g/1 lb 2 oz spaghetti*

1/2 green chilli

Tablespoon/teaspoon
Sharp knife
Sieve or colander
2 frying-pans (if possible)
Kitchen paper
Plate
Large saucepan

• METHOD •

1 Wash the aubergine, trim the ends, and chop into sticks 2–2.5 cm/3/4–1 inch long and 8 mm/1/4 inch wide (cut into 2–2.5 cm slices and cross-chop). Sprinkle with fine salt and put into a sieve or colander to sweat for 30 mins–1 hour. Rinse under the cold tap and leave in the sieve or colander to drain.
2 Trim the leaf and root ends of the celery; wash, dry, and slice finely. Peel and finely chop the onion and garlic, keeping each separate. Skin and chop the tomatoes, throwing away the hard cores. Wash, dry, and halve the chilli; wrap the half which is not needed in foodwrap and store in the refrigerator. Discard the stalk, inner membrane and all the seeds, and dice finely. Do not rub your eyes while preparing it, and wash your hands directly afterwards. Finely grate the cheese.
3 If you have only one pan, fry the aubergine; otherwise, wait until the sauce has simmered 20 minutes (see Step 4). If necessary, blot the aubergine dry with kitchen paper; season lightly with salt and moderately with pepper. Set a plate conveniently to hand near the cooker. Warm 2 1/2 tablespoonsful of oil over high heat, add the aubergine, and stir-fry 4–4 1/2 minutes, until it is deep golden brown on all sides (except the skin). Transfer to the plate.
4 Put 1 tablespoonful of oil into the pan and fry the onion and celery over low heat for 5 minutes, turning often. Add the garlic and fry for another 5 minutes. Add the chilli and fry, turning constantly, for 3–5 minutes, or until the celery is soft and the onion soft but not brown. Add the tomatoes and season lightly with salt and pepper; stir in the sugar. Simmer for 7–10 minutes, pressing the lumps of tomato flesh against the bottom

of the pan until liquefied. Stir in the purée and simmer over very low heat for 25 minutes. If the aubergine is already fried, stir it in and simmer 3–4 minutes more; if not, stir-fry it after the sauce has simmered for 20 minutes, add it, and simmer for a further 2–3 minutes.

5 Set the water to boil for the spaghetti (see pages 50–1 for cooking time) while the sauce simmers.

6 Drain the cooked pasta and toss it with the cheese.

7 Either toss some of the sauce into the spaghetti or serve the sauce on top.

• Spaghetti with Olive and Tomato Sauce •

This can be served with spaghetti or bucatini, but as tomatoes and olives are a fairly powerful combination, it also goes well with thick, chunky pasta such as rigatoni.

Use black olives preserved in brine: green ones, which are picked before the fruit is fully ripe, are too sharp. Pitted ones save time but are not so succulent and tend to have less flavour than whole ones.

As the dish contains no high-protein ingredient, either serve with grated Parmesan or make up the deficiency at another meal. *For* 4.

• INGREDIENTS •

2 sticks celery (not from the outside)

1 medium onion

3 cloves garlic

750 g/1 lb 8 oz ripe tomatoes

1/2 green chilli

100 g/3 1/2 oz black olives

1 tablespoonful olive oil

Salt

Pepper

1 teaspoonful soft brown sugar

1 tablespoonful tomato purée

500 g/1 lb 2 oz spaghetti

Tablespoon
Teaspoon
Sharp knife
Frying-pan
Spatula
Large saucepan

• METHOD •

1 Trim the leaf and root ends from the celery and remove any discoloured streaks; wash, dry, and slice finely. Peel and finely chop the onion and garlic; skin and chop the tomatoes. Wash, dry, and halve the chilli. (You can store the unused half, wrapped in foodwrap, in the refrigerator.) Trim the stalk if necessary from the half you are going to use, remove the inner membrane and seeds, and dice as finely as possible. Do not rub your eyes while chopping it and wash your hands immediately afterwards. Drain and chop the olives.

2 Fry the onion and celery in the oil over low heat for 5 minutes, turning often; add the garlic and fry for another 5 minutes. Add the chilli and fry 3–5 minutes or until the celery is soft and the onion soft but not brown; turn constantly. Add the tomatoes, season lightly with salt and pepper, stir in the sugar, and simmer 7–10 minutes, pressing the lumps of flesh against the bottom of the pan until dissolved. Stir in the purée, add the olives, and simmer 25 minutes.

3 Set the water to boil for the pasta while the sauce is simmering (see pages 50–1 for cooking time).

4 When pasta is cooked, drain it, then toss some of the sauce into the pasta before serving; place the rest on top.

• Capricciosa or Spaghetti • with Aubergine and Walnut

Here, the richness of the crisply fried aubergine is emphasized by the even crisper nuts.

The dish is very simple: just for this reason, however, the quality of the ingredients is especially important. If possible, buy freshly made capricciosa (semolina and egg noodles); otherwise, use a good brand of dried spaghetti. Similarly, choose really hard, fresh aubergines; spongy or wrinkled ones will be old and tend to become mushy when fried.

The quantities given are really enough for three, but the aubergine is so good that it seems a pity to be mean with it; I have not given enough for more because this is as much as will fit comfortably into a large wok or frying-pan (one of the advantages of cutting it into chunks rather than the more conventional slices is that with slices you would have to fry it in two sessions). It is particularly important to allow it to sweat for at least half an hour before starting to cook because this makes it less absorbent and thus reduces the amount of oil needed (you will need less if you use a non-stick pan).

Serve with finely grated pecorino. *For 2.*

• INGREDIENTS •

500 g/1 lb 2 oz aubergine (1 large or 2 medium to small)

Fine salt

Bunch of parsley (enough for 2 tablespoonsful when chopped)

50 g/2 oz walnuts or walnut pieces

5 cloves garlic

50 g/2 oz butter

Pepper

2½–3½ tablespoonsful olive oil

250 g/9 oz capricciosa or spaghetti

Non-stick wok or frying-pan (if possible)
Sharp knife
Spatula
Tablespoon
Large plate
Kitchen paper
Large saucepan
Colander

• METHOD •

1 Wash the aubergine(s); chop off the stalk end and cut into chunks about 2.5 cm/1 inch long, 1.5 cm/2/3 inch wide, and of about the same thickness as width. Sprinkle the slices with fine salt and leave to sweat in a colander for 1/2–1 hour. Rinse under the cold tap and turn on to a large plate lined with kitchen paper to dry.

2 Wash the parsley and trim the ends; shake off surplus water, blot dry with kitchen paper, and chop finely. Chop or coarsely crush the nuts. Peel and slice 3 of the cloves of garlic fairly finely.

3 Peel, roughly chop, and crush the remaining 2 cloves of garlic in a mortar. Add and crush the parsley. Chop the butter into small squares and add. Season with a little salt and pepper (you will need very little salt if you are using salted butter) and pound to a paste.

4 Set the water to boil for the pasta (see pages 50–1 for cooking time). Time it to be ready 7 minutes after you start frying the aubergine.

5 Check that the aubergine is dry and if necessary blot with more kitchen paper. Warm 2 1/2 tablespoonsful of oil over medium heat in the wok or frying-pan. Add the slices of garlic and allow them to fry until starting to change colour; remove from the pan and set aside. Put in the aubergine, season moderately with salt and pepper, and fry, turning constantly, 5–6 minutes or until it is pale brown on all sides (except the skin). Add the nuts and turn briefly in the oil. Remove from the heat, continuing to turn for a moment or two while the pan cools.

6 When the pasta is cooked, drain it, and toss it with the parsley butter. Return the aubergine and nuts to the heat, add the lightly coloured slices of garlic, and fry, turning continuously, until the aubergine is rich brown and the nuts are also beginning to brown. Empty the contents of the pan at once over the pasta; mix and serve.

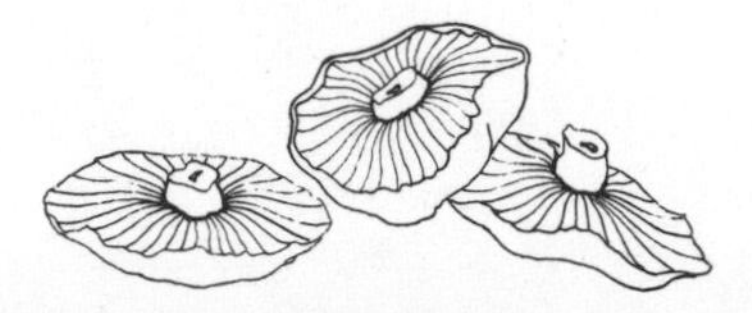

• Tagliatelle with • Mushroom and Porcini Sauce

Porcini are dried wild Italian mushrooms with a very pronounced and (I think) completely delicious flavour. Although they are expensive, only a few are needed to give a dish zest and character. You may not be able to buy them in the local supermarket but they will be stocked at Italian grocers or delicatessens.

I suggest accompanying them with a mixture of button and flat mushrooms, the first specifically for their texture and the second for flavour.

The dish is quick to prepare and cook but the porcini need soaking for 20–25 minutes.

Serve with plain, maize or garlic and herb tagliatelle. You do not need cheese with the sauce; egg pasta is therefore particularly desirable, since otherwise the dish will contain no high-protein ingredient. *For* 4.

• INGREDIENTS •

10 g/⅓ oz (1 small packet) porcini
200 g/7 oz button mushrooms
200 g/7 oz large mushrooms
4 cloves garlic
20 g/¾ oz butter
Salt
Pepper
2 tablespoonsful olive oil
4 tablespoonsful double cream
500 g/1 lb 2 oz tagliatelle

Tablespoon
2 bowls
Sharp knife
Kitchen paper
Wok or frying-pan
Large saucepan
Spatula
Colander

• METHOD •

1 Cover the porcini with hot (not boiling) water and leave them to soak for 20–25 minutes. Trim the stems of the fresh mushrooms. Wash and dry the button ones; peel, wash, and dry the larger ones. Halve or quarter the larger ones according to size and slice all of them about 6 mm/less than 1/4 inch thick. Peel and finely slice 3 of the cloves of garlic.

2 Peel and roughly chop the remaining clove of garlic; roughly chop the butter. Crush the garlic in a mortar; add the butter with a moderate seasoning of salt and pepper (less salt if the butter is heavily salted) and pound to a paste.

3 Drain the porcini over a bowl; keep the soaking-liquor and add it to the water in which you cook the pasta. Blot the porcini dry with kitchen paper; chop up any large pieces.

4 Put the porcini into a wok or frying-pan with the other mushrooms and the sliced garlic. Season with a little salt and slightly more pepper and fry over low heat, turning often, 8–10 minutes or until soft and the fresh mushrooms have started to exude juice. Remove from the heat.

5 While the mushrooms fry, set the water to boil for the pasta (see pages 50–1 for cooking time).

6 About 1 1/2 minutes before the pasta is ready, return the mushrooms to the heat. Add the garlic butter and, as soon as it has melted, the cream. Bring just to the boil and turn off the heat. Drain the pasta and toss with some of the sauce; serve the rest on top.

• TRENETTE OR TAGLIATELLE WITH • PESTO, GREEN BEANS AND POTATOES

Next to tomato and perhaps Bolognese, pesto is deservedly the most famous of all pasta sauces; less well known, however, is that the traditional way to serve it is not with pasta alone but with pasta mixed with beans and potatoes. When you try it this way, you will see why: the taste of the beans, and the smoothness of the potatoes set off its pungency and nutty texture perfectly.

Happily, so far as this book is concerned, pesto is much better made with a pestle and mortar than with a blender: this applies to almost all sauces containing nuts, where an uneven texture is an advantage, but in this instance pounding also draws out the juices and hence the flavour of the basil much more effectively than blending.

Both basil and pine nuts are expensive and sometimes difficult to buy. As I have said elsewhere (see page 7), it is a good idea to grow your own basil; without it, however, you can make Parsley Pesto (see page 65); similarly, pine nuts can be replaced by walnuts, which give a rather different but still excellent result (other nuts are less successful, but almost any can be used for Parsley Pesto).

The crispness of small Kenya or French beans is desirable, but green haricots, which are larger and cheaper, can also be used, provided they are fresh. Old, flaccid ones will take longer to cook, which particularly matters in this instance because I have suggested boiling them with the pasta. This is not the best way to cook them, since they should be covered with the minimum of water, but it avoids the need for using three saucepans. (You can of course boil them separately if you prefer.)

It is important to use waxy new potatoes, e.g. Pentland Javelin, Ulster Sceptre, or Maris Bard, since floury ones may simply crumble into the pasta and beans. (Cold waxy potatoes with pesto, incidentally, make an excellent salad.)

The traditional kind of pasta for this dish is trenette, which is narrower than tagliatelle, but tagliatelle goes with it almost, if not quite, as well: if you are using home-made pasta, choose plain, tomato, or maize.

If you have both, use a mixture of Parmesan and pecorino cheeses.

With walnuts instead of pine nuts, you will need a little more oil.

Serve with extra Parmesan or pecorino. *For 2–3.*

• INGREDIENTS •

3–4 sprigs parsley

About 24 basil leaves

3 tablespoonsful olive oil (with pine nuts) or 4 tablespoonsful (with walnuts)

20 g/¾ oz each Parmesan *and pecorino cheese, or 40 g/1½ oz of one or the other*

1 large, 1½ medium, or 2 small cloves garlic

40 g/1½ oz pine nuts or walnuts

Salt

375 g/13 oz waxy new potatoes

200 g/7 oz Kenya, French, *or green haricot beans*

250 g/9 oz trenette or tagliatelle

Tablespoon
Sharp knife
Kitchen paper
Grater (optional)
Pestle and mortar
1 medium, 1 large saucepan
Colander

• METHOD •

1 Make the pesto. Trim the stems of the parsley. Wash the parsley and basil leaves, blot dry with kitchen paper, and chop finely. Finely grate the cheese(s) if necessary. Peel and roughly chop the garlic. Crush the garlic in a mortar. Add and crush the nuts; add and pound the parsley and basil. Stir in the oil. Add a pinch of salt and the cheese and mix to a paste.

2 Scrub the potatoes and remove any eyes or green patches. Just cover them with slightly salted water, bring to the boil, and boil 15–20 minutes, until the potatoes are tender but still firm; drain.

3 While the potatoes cook, top and tail the beans and cut into shortish lengths. Put them into a large saucepan three-quarters filled with water; add a teaspoonful of salt and a drop of oil. Set on the heat when the potatoes have been boiling for 15 minutes. Bring to the boil and boil the Kenya beans for 2 minutes, haricots for 3. Add the pasta, cook for 4 minutes, or until it is just tender, and drain.

4 Slice the potatoes as soon as they are cool enough to handle. Mix the cooked, drained pasta and beans with about half the pesto. Place in the serving-bowls with a well in the middle. Pile the slices of potato into the well and top with a generous blob of the remaining pesto. Serve at once.

• TAGLIATELLE OR TAGLIOLINI • WITH PARSLEY PESTO

This is the perfect sauce: it is cheap, quick, and easy, can be prepared ahead of time, and I think is quite as delicious in its own way as the traditional sort of pesto made with basil (see page 62). The idea of it comes from the chef Carla Tomasi, now the principal of a cookery school, who made it with almonds to accompany ravioli; it is just as good with tagliatelle or tagliolini, however, especially home-made, and you can use almost any sort of nut. Personally, I like it best with almonds, but only by a narrow margin: peanuts and hazelnuts are also excellent, walnuts very good, and cashews particularly rich and creamy. Peanuts need toasting in the oven; almonds and hazelnuts are slightly better toasted, although I am not sure that it is worth turning on the oven specially; cashews and walnuts are definitely better untoasted.

Take care to use the right amount of garlic, since with too little the sauce will be dull and with too much, burningly strong.

If possible, use unskinned almonds or hazelnuts, since skinned ones will have lost much of their flavour and succulence.

Make the sauce (which except for toasting nuts is uncooked) before boiling the pasta.

Serve with plain, brown, or herb tagliatelle or tagliolini and grated pecorino cheese. *For 2.*

• INGREDIENTS •

50 g/2 oz peanuts, cashew nuts, walnuts, or unskinned almonds or hazelnuts

Bunch parsley (enough for 2 tablespoonsful when chopped)

1 large, 2 small, or 1 1/2 medium cloves garlic

25 g/1 oz pecorino cheese

3 tablespoonsful olive oil

A little extra olive oil (optional)

250 g/9 oz tagliatelle or tagliolini

Tablespoon
Sharp knife
Pestle and mortar
Grater
Bowl
Kitchen paper
Large saucepan
Colander
Small baking-tray (optional)

• METHOD •

1 If you are using peanuts, or wish to toast almonds or hazelnuts, set the oven to 200°C, 400°F, Gas Mark 6. Spread the nuts on the baking-tray and toast peanuts for 8–10 minutes, hazelnuts for 10–12 minutes, and almonds for 14–16 minutes, or in all cases until the nuts are just starting to brown.
2 Trim the stalks, wash and thoroughly dry the parsley by squeezing in kitchen paper. Chop as finely as possible. Set the water to boil for the pasta (see pages 50–1 for cooking time).
3 Peel, slice, and crush the garlic in a mortar. Add and slightly crush the parsley. Add and crush the nuts to about the fineness of coarse breadcrumbs, leaving a few larger pieces (an uneven texture adds interest to the dish).
4 Finely grate the cheese if necessary; stir into the mixture with the oil.
5 When the pasta is cooked, drain and toss with the sauce.

• Spaghetti with • Red Pepper Sauce

This is pungent and rich-tasting: particularly if the tomatoes are a little sharp, the sweetness of the peppers gives it an almost sweet-and-sour quality. It is a classic Italian sauce but usually served with roast or grilled meat rather than pasta. One way to eat it would be with pork chops or lamb accompanied by tagliatelle instead of potatoes; however, it is also excellent on its own with flat pasta or spaghetti.

It will cost least if you make it in the autumn, when peppers and tomatoes are cheapest.

Choose firm, glossy peppers and fairly firm tomatoes: hard, unripe ones, which would add to the sour element in the flavour, will not be juicy enough to give a moist consistency.

The strong flavour of the sauce means that you will not need cheese, but bear in mind that in itself it contains no high-protein ingredient: unless you eat it with home-made tagliatelle or meat, the deficiency should be made up for at another time. *For 3 or 4; if served with meat, 4–5.*

• INGREDIENTS •

500 g/1 lb 2 oz moderately ripe tomatoes

2 medium onions

3 cloves garlic

375 g/13 oz (2 large or 3 small) red peppers

1 green, or green and red, chilli

2 tablespoonsful olive oil or, if necessary, a little more

Salt

Pepper

1 tablespoonful tomato purée

375 g/13 oz or 500 g/1 lb 2 oz spaghetti

Sharp knife
Frying-pan
Tablespoon
Large saucepan

• METHOD •

1 Skin and chop the tomatoes, throwing away the hard cores. Peel and slice the onions into fine rings; peel and finely chop the garlic. Wash, dry, and quarter the peppers. Remove the pith and all the seeds; cut out any dark spots or soft patches (if the peppers are fresh, there will not be any). Halve the quarters of large peppers lengthwise so that when you slice across you will not end up with very long strips; cut the pieces across into slices about 8 mm/¼ inch wide. Wash, dry, and finely dice the chilli; do not rub your eyes while handling it and wash your hands immediately afterwards.

2 Fry the onion in 2 tablespoonsful of oil over moderately low

heat for 5 minutes, turning often; add the pepper and fry for 5 more. Add the garlic and continue to fry for 10 minutes, turning constantly; add the chilli and cook for a further 3–4 minutes or until the onions and pepper are very soft but have not quite begun to change colour. Add the tomatoes and turn down the heat to very low. Season with a little salt and rather more pepper and simmer, pressing the lumps of tomato flesh against the bottom of the pan, for 10 minutes or until they have liquefied. Stir in the tomato purée and simmer for 15–20 minutes. Turn fairly often and keep an eye on the contents of the pan: the sauce is intended to be fairly thick but not dry. If necessary, add a little extra oil.
3 Start cooking the pasta (see pages 50–1 for cooking time) while the sauce is simmering. When the pasta is cooked, drain, and toss with some of the sauce; serve the rest on top.

• Conchiglie or Tagliatelle • with Broccoli and Pepper

This is not a traditional Italian sauce; something like it was suggested to me by the chef Carla Tomasi, but she browns the broccoli as well as the garlic and her version does not include pepper. It is much more special than its simplicity suggests: it is essential, however, to fry the garlic and pepper until they are really brown and blackening respectively.

Besides conchiglie, you can make it with penne, macaroni, or home-made brown or wholemeal tagliatelle, which to my surprise I found best of all. Home-made pasta is also a good idea because it provides egg: otherwise, the only high-protein ingredient in the dish is the cheese.

Make sure that the broccoli is hard and crisp, with a clean rather than pronounced broccoli smell; the pepper should also be hard and glossy. The vegetables take 5–6 minutes to cook: if you are using conchiglie (shells) or other short pasta, start frying them when the pasta has 6 minutes to boil. If necessary, reheat the vegetables by stir-frying them for a few seconds.

Serve with a little more cheese. *For 2 or 3.*

• INGREDIENTS •

250 g/9 oz broccoli, or 200 g/7 oz if it is bought already trimmed into florets

1 large red pepper

4 large or 5 small cloves of garlic

1/2 chilli (any)

40–50 g/1 1/2–2 oz pecorino cheese

2 tablespoonsful olive oil plus a little more for drizzling

250 g/9 oz or 375 g/13 oz conchiglie or tagliatelle

Tablespoon
Sharp knife
Saucepan
Sieve or colander
Bowl
Grater (optional)
Wok or frying-pan
Large saucepan

• METHOD •

1 Wash the broccoli and trim it into florets 2.5 cm/1 inch long, 2–2.5 cm/3/4 inch wide at the flower end, and 8 mm/1/4 inch thick at the stalk end. Just cover it with slightly salted water, bring to the boil, and boil 3 minutes. Drain in a sieve set over a bowl to catch the cooking liquor. Rinse under the cold tap and leave to dry. Add the liquor to the water in which you boil the pasta.

2 Wash, dry, and quarter the pepper. Throw away the core and all the seeds and trim off the white inner membrane and any dark spots. Cut it into strips 8 mm/1/4 inch wide and 2.5–3 cm/1–1 1/4 inch long. Peel and finely slice the garlic. Wash and dry the chilli. Trim the stalk end, slit it in half, and remove the seeds. (With a fresh one, wrap the half you do not need in foodwrap and store it in the refrigerator; return the spare half of a dried one to its container – but make sure that it is perfectly dry.) Dice as finely as possible. Do not rub your eyes while chopping and wash your hands afterwards. Grate the cheese if necessary.

3 Set the water to boil for the pasta (see pages 50–1 for cooking time). Put in short pasta. Start cooking tagliatelle when the vegetables have been frying 10 minutes.

4 Put the olive oil and pepper into a wok or frying-pan. Fry over medium to high heat, stirring often, for 1½ minutes; add the garlic and fry for 2 more minutes, until the pepper begins to blacken. Add the broccoli and chilli and stir-fry for 2 minutes or until the pepper is partly blackened and the broccoli crisp and just beginning to change colour. Remove from the heat, continuing to stir for a few seconds while the oil cools.

5 When the pasta is cooked, drain, and quickly toss with the cheese. Drizzle with a little extra oil; serve the pepper and broccoli on top.

• Spaghetti or Tagliolini • with Mushroom Sauce and Basil Butter

This is a very quick, simple sauce: it takes only a few minutes to prepare and 8–10 to cook.

Use large, open mushrooms, which generally have more flavour than button ones and will yield more juice. Check that they are fresh: they should be firm and hard, including the gills. A distinctive smell of mushroom is also an indication of freshness. The addition of prawns is optional. Unshelled ones have more taste and a drier, firmer texture than shelled ones; if you use frozen ones, they will take several hours to defrost.

Serve with spaghetti or tagliolini and plenty of grated Parmesan cheese (if you are not adding prawns). *For 4 with prawns, or 3 without.*

• INGREDIENTS •

250 g/9 oz unshelled or 125 g/4 oz shelled prawns (optional) or 60 g/2 oz grated Parmesan

375 g/13 oz large mushrooms

24–30 basil leaves

40 g/1½ oz butter

Pepper

Salt

2–3 tablespoonsful olive oil

5 cloves garlic

375 g/13 oz or 500 g/1 lb 2 oz spaghetti or tagliolini

Tablespoon
Sharp knife
Kitchen paper
Pestle and mortar
Large saucepan
Colander

• METHOD •

1 Shell the prawns if necessary: pull off the heads and gently pull the shell from the tail. Pick off the rest of the shell with your fingers. Drain frozen prawns. Grate the Parmesan.
2 Trim the ends of the mushroom stalks. Wash the mushrooms and blot dry with kitchen paper. If the stalks are very thick, pull them off and chop them separately. Slice the mushrooms finely; halve the slices of very large ones.
3 Wash and thoroughly dry the basil leaves; tear into small pieces and put them into a mortar. Peel the garlic and finely slice 4 of the cloves. Roughly chop the 5th and add it to the mortar. Crush it with the basil to a paste. Chop the butter into small squares and add. Season moderately with pepper and moderately or very lightly with salt according to whether the butter is salted. Pound until thoroughly mixed.
4 Set the water to boil for the pasta (see pages 50–1 for cooking time). Start cooking spaghetti before starting to fry the mushrooms; do not put in tagliolini until you are ready to heat the prawns .
5 Fry the rest of the garlic in the oil over medium heat 1–2 minutes or until just starting to change colour. Reduce the heat to low and add the mushrooms. Fry gently, turning often, 5–7 minutes or until soft and beginning to exude juice. Add the prawns and continue frying 1–2 minutes, until they are thoroughly heated but still soft (as they are almost always sold ready-boiled, they only need heating rather than cooking: if cooked for long, they will become tough).
6 When the pasta is cooked, drain and (if not adding prawns) toss with the cheese. Stir the basil butter into the mushrooms, toss with the pasta and serve at once.

• Spaghetti or Tagliatelle with • Anchovy, Olive, and Tomato Sauce

This is based on a classic Neapolitan sauce which also contains capers. Traditionally, it is served with spaghetti, but it can also be served with home-made tagliatelle: as it is already very piquant, it does not need cheese, for which reason it goes particularly well with brown or wholemeal pasta. *For* 3 *or* 4.

• INGREDIENTS •

750 g/1 lb 8 oz ripe tomatoes
1 largish onion
3 cloves garlic
8 anchovy fillets (1 tin)
100 g/3½ oz black olives
Small bunch parsley
1 small or ½ larger dried chilli
1 tablespoonful olive oil
1½ tablespoonsful tomato purée
1 level teaspoonful soft brown sugar
Pepper
375 g/13 oz or 500 g/1 lb 2 oz spaghetti or tagliatelle

Saucepan
Tablespoon
Teaspoon
Sharp knife
Kitchen paper
Frying-pan
Spatula
Large saucepan
Colander

• METHOD •

1 Skin and chop the tomatoes, discarding the hard cores. Peel and finely chop the onion and garlic. Finely chop the anchovies, keeping a little of their oil; stone and chop the olives. Wash and blot the parsley dry with kitchen paper. Chop it finely. Wash and dry the chilli; remove the stalk end, slit it, and take out all the seeds. (If you are using only half, return the other half to its container, but ensure that it is thoroughly dry.) Dice as finely as possible. Do not rub your eyes while handling it and wash your hands directly afterwards.

2 Fry the onion in the oil over low heat, turning often, for 8–10 minutes or until soft but not brown. Turn up the heat to medium and add the garlic; fry for about 2 minutes and add the chilli, anchovies, olives, and parsley. Continue frying, turning continuously, for another minute or until the garlic is starting to change colour. Add the tomatoes, lower the heat, and simmer until they have dissolved, pressing the flesh against the bottom and sides of the pan. Add the tomato purée, sugar, and a moderate sprinkling of pepper, and continue to simmer for 25 minutes, stirring from time to time.

3 Start cooking spaghetti while the sauce simmers (see pages 50–1); do not put in tagliatelle until the sauce is almost ready.

4 When the pasta is cooked, drain, and either toss with some of the sauce or serve the sauce on top.

• Tagliatelle with Spinach, • Anchovy, Nuts and Sultanas

This is a particularly successful combination of flavours: the bitterness of the spinach and saltiness of the anchovies are offset by the sudden sweetness of the sultanas. Texture is added by the nuts and crisply fried slices of garlic. Except in that the authentic version is made with pine nuts, it is a traditional Genoese dish: because pine nuts are disproportionately expensive, I have replaced them with peanuts (I have also on occasion used almonds, which are acceptable but a little sweet).

Ideally, choose spinach which has been pulled up by the root, since it is usually in better condition than individual leaves; because it is easier to pick over, it is also quicker to prepare. Sometimes a similar vegetable with bigger leaves and thick white stems is sold instead: this is beet spinach, or sea-kale beet, which can be used for this recipe but does not have quite the same flavour.

Serve with tagliatelle or tagliolini/tagliarini. With the saltiness of the anchovies, you will not need cheese: partly for this reason, the sauce goes particularly well with brown or wholemeal pasta. *For* 3.

• INGREDIENTS •

25 *g*/1 *oz sultanas*

500 *g*/1 *lb* 2 *oz spinach or sea-kale beet*

Salt

3 *large or* 4 *small cloves garlic*

8 *anchovy fillets* (1 *tin*)

25 *g*/1 *oz plain peanuts* (*or pine nuts or almonds*)

2 *tablespoonsful olive oil*

15 *g*/½ *oz butter*

375 *g*/13 *oz tagliatelle*

Largish saucepan with a lid
Fish-slice or slotted spoon (if possible)
Tablespoon
Teaspoon
Bowl
Kitchen paper
Sharp knife
Colander or sieve
Pestle and mortar

• METHOD •

1 Separate any sultanas which have stuck together and soak in warm water for 15 minutes. Drain and dry on kitchen paper.

2 Remove roots and any weeds or damaged leaves from the spinach and wash, twice if necessary. Put into the largish saucepan with 1 tablespoonful water and ½ teaspoonful salt. Cover and set over medium heat for 4 minutes. Stir, and boil 1–2 minutes more or until submerged in juice and tender. Remove from the heat and drain: press out as much liquid as you can with the back of a tablespoon and chop finely.

To prepare sea-kale beet, remove the thick part of the stems, which takes longer to cook than the leaves: cut or tear up each side as far as necessary. Wash and put the leaves into the saucepan with about an inch of water in the bottom and 1/2 teaspoonful salt, as above. Cover, and cook 5 minutes; stir, and cook another 2 minutes or until the leaves have collapsed and are tender. Drain and chop as for spinach. (If you want to utilize the pieces of stem, wash and chop them into short lengths and add them to Bean and Macaroni Soup (see page 43) or stir-fried vegetables. They take 9–10 minutes to simmer and 2–3 to stir-fry.)

3 Peel and slice the garlic fairly finely. Drain the anchovies of most of their oil and dice; coarsely crush the nuts.

4 Set the water to boil for the pasta (see pages 50–1 for cooking time). Since tagliatelle usually take only 4 minutes to cook, do not put them in until you have fried and removed the garlic for the sauce (see below).

5 In a frying-pan, melt the butter in the oil over medium to highish heat. Add the garlic and allow to fry 30 seconds or until an even pale brown. Remove the pan from the heat, take out the garlic chips with the slotted spoon or fish-slice (or, if you do not have one, an ordinary spoon), and set them near to hand. Return the pan to the heat and add the anchovy. Fry, pressing the pieces against the bottom of the pan, for 40–60 seconds or until they have disintegrated in the oil. Add the nuts and toss in the oil and anchovy mixture. Turn the spinach into the pan and stir 1–1 1/2 minutes, until thoroughly mixed and hot; do not leave it to fry longer or it will taste twice-cooked. Stir in the garlic and sultanas, and cook for a few seconds to warm them through completely.

6 When the pasta is cooked, drain and serve with the spinach on top of the pasta.

• Spaghetti with Stir-fried • Mushrooms and Prawns

This is very simple and fairly quick to prepare – how quick being in inverse proportion to the quality of the ingredients: unfortunately, as the aim is that the prawns should be juicy and the mushrooms crisp, unshelled prawns and small button mushrooms, which take a bit longer to trim and wash than larger ones, are the ideal. If you use frozen prawns, remember to allow several hours for them to defrost.

With the prawns, and as the dish is very garlicky, you will not want to add cheese. *For* 2.

• INGREDIENTS •

Bunch parsley (enough for 2 tablespoonsful when chopped)

5–6 cloves garlic

40 g/1 1/2 oz butter

Pepper

Salt

250 g/9 oz small button mushrooms

250 g/9 oz unshelled or 125 g/4 oz shelled prawns

1/2 green chilli

2 tablespoonsful olive oil

250 g/9 oz spaghetti

Tablespoon
Sharp knife
Kitchen paper
Pestle and mortar
Colander (optional)
Plate
Wok or frying-pan
Spatula

• METHOD •

1 Trim the ends of the parsley. Wash it, blot dry with kitchen paper, and chop finely. Peel the garlic; roughly chop 1 large or 1 1/2 medium cloves and crush in a mortar. Finely slice the rest and set aside. Add the parsley to the mortar and crush thoroughly. Unless it is already soft, chop the butter into smallish squares; add to the mortar with a moderate seasoning of pepper and a little salt (very little, if the butter is heavily salted). Pound to a paste: it should be a light but quite bright green, dotted with darker flecks of parsley.

2 Trim the mushroom stalks; wash, dry, and finely slice the mushrooms. Peel unshelled prawns (see page 71). Rinse ready-shelled ones under the cold tap; drain frozen ones. In both cases, set on a plate lined with kitchen paper to dry. Wash and dry the chilli; remove the stalk end and slit in half. (Wrap the half which is not needed in foodwrap and store in the refrigerator.) Remove the seeds and inner membrane and dice as finely as possible. Do not rub your eyes while handling it and wash your hands immediately afterwards.

3 Set the spaghetti to boil (see pages 50–1 for cooking time); time it to be ready 4 minutes after you start to fry.

4 Season the mushrooms lightly with salt and pepper. Warm the oil in a wok or frying-pan over high heat. Add the sliced garlic and allow it to fry 30 seconds or until starting to colour. Add the mushrooms and stir-fry 2 minutes; add the chilli and stir-fry 1/2–1 minute or until the mushrooms begin to turn gold at the edges. Add the prawns, stir for 1/2 minute, and remove from the heat.

5 When the pasta is cooked, drain it and either toss the prawns and mushrooms into it or serve the pasta and place them on top. Put a generous dollop of the green parsley and garlic butter in the centre of each serving.

• Spaghetti or Tagliatelle • with Ragu Bolognese

This is the sauce used for spaghetti Bolognese, although in fact it is traditionally served with fresh tagliatelle. Far from being merely a sauce of minced beef, the authentic version is an example of how long, slow cooking can completely transform ingredients, all of which (except wine, which is far from essential) are in this instance of a very ordinary kind.

Wine is always included in the authentic versions, but when served as a sauce the following seems to me to be all that one could wish without it; the recipe can also be used as a filling for lasagne (see page 126), when, however, the additional strength of flavour given by the wine is an improvement, although still very optional. The really important point about the ragu is that it should be simmered for the full 2 1/2 hours: cooked for less time, it is just meat sauce.

It can be made a day in advance but needs reheating carefully.

Serve with spaghetti or plain tagliatelle and grated Parmesan or pecorino. *For* 4.

• INGREDIENTS •

1 medium onion
1 stick celery
125 g/4½ oz unsmoked streaky bacon
1 carrot
3 cloves garlic
Sprig rosemary (optional, but very desirable)
375 g/13 oz ripe tomatoes
1 tablespoonful olive oil
250 g/9 oz lean, finely minced beef
Salt
Pepper
4 tablespoonsful red wine (very optional)
¾ teaspoonful soft dark brown sugar
150 ml/¼ pint milk, plus a little extra if necessary
1½ tablespoonsful tomato purée
500 g/1 lb 2 oz spaghetti or tagliatelle

Tablespoon
Teaspoon
Sharp knife
Scissors
Frying-pan
Spatula
Large saucepan

• METHOD •

1 Peel and finely chop the onion. Discard the leaf and root end of the celery, pare off any brownish streaks, and slice finely. Remove the rind and any bone from the bacon and dice (use scissors). Peel and finely slice the carrot; peel and finely chop the garlic. Keep the carrot and garlic apart from the other prepared ingredients. Wash the rosemary; skin and chop the tomatoes, discarding the cores.

2 Fry the onion, celery, and bacon in the oil over very low heat, turning now and again, for 5 minutes. Add the carrot and garlic and continue to fry, turning often, for 8–10 minutes: pull the leaves from the stem of rosemary, add, and fry 3–5 minutes more or until the celery is soft and the onion soft but not brown. Add the beef, season lightly with salt and pepper, and fry, turning continuously and pressing the meat against the bottom of the pan, until all parts of it are brown rather than red. Do not, however, fry it until dark brown: it should be only lightly seared. Add the wine if you are using it and simmer for 10 minutes or until it has cooked away. Add the tomatoes and season again with a little salt and pepper; stir in the sugar and continue to cook, pressing the lumps of tomato flesh against the sides and bottom of the pan, for 7–10 minutes or until liquefied. Add the milk and simmer 15–20 minutes. Stir in the tomato purée and simmer as slowly as possible for 2½ hours. The surface of the sauce should barely move. If it seems dry, add a little extra milk.

3 If you are making it in advance, allow to cool, cover, and store in the refrigerator. Reheat for 7–10 minutes over the lowest possible heat, as it was cooked; stir frequently. Add a very little milk if necessary. If you are eating it immediately, set the water to boil for the pasta towards the end of the simmering (see pages 50–1 for cooking time).

4 To serve, drain the cooked pasta and toss with some or all of the sauce.

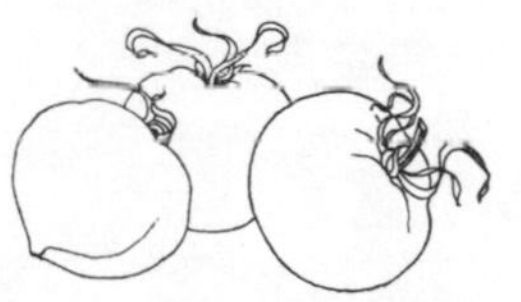

• Bucatini with Bacon • and Tomato Sauce

This is my adaptation of a sauce said to have originated at the small town of Amatrice in Italy. The bacon should be crisp and the celery chunky. Cooking the ingredients in the melted bacon fat adds considerably to the flavour.

The sauce is customarily served with spaghetti or bucatini, which is slightly thicker than spaghetti and particularly suits its robust character.

Grated pecorino is tossed into the pasta before serving: accompany it with more if you wish. *For* 4.

• INGREDIENTS •

250 *g*/9 *oz unsmoked streaky bacon*

1 *medium onion*

750 *g*/1 *lb* 8 *oz ripe tomatoes*

1 *large (but not outside) stick celery*

½ *green chilli*

1 *dessertspoonful olive oil*

Salt

Pepper

1 *teaspoonful soft brown sugar*

1½ *tablespoonsful tomato purée*

60 *g*/*generous* 2 *oz finely grated pecorino*

500 *g*/1 *lb* 2 *oz spaghetti or bucatini*

Fish-slice or perforated spoon
Tablespoon, Dessertspoon, Teaspoon
Scissors
Sharp knife
Frying-pan
Spatula
Plate
Large saucepan
Colander

• METHOD •

1 Trim the rind and any bone from the bacon and cut into 1.5 cm/⅔ inch squares (use scissors). Peel and finely chop the onion; skin and chop the tomatoes, throwing away the hard cores. Trim the leaf and root end of the celery; pare off any brownish streaks, wash, dry, and slice finely. Wash, dry, and slit the chilli, removing the stalk; wrap the half which you will not need in foodwrap and store in the refrigerator. Remove the seeds and inner membrane and dice as finely as possible. Do not touch your eyes while handling it and wash your hands directly afterwards.

2 Fry the bacon in the oil over medium heat for 8–10 minutes or until crisp and the fat gold: stir continuously at the beginning to ensure that the pieces do not stick together, and frequently thereafter. Transfer the bacon to a plate with the fish-slice or perforated spoon, leaving the fat behind in the pan.

3 Reduce the heat to low and fry the onion and celery in the bacon fat, turning often, for 8–10 minutes. Add the chilli and continue frying for 3–5 minutes or until the celery is soft and the onion soft but not brown. Add the tomato, season lightly with salt and moderately with pepper, and simmer 7–10 minutes or until liquefied, pressing the flesh against the bottom of the pan. Stir in the sugar and tomato purée and simmer for 25 minutes.

4 Grate the cheese if necessary.

5 Set the spaghetti or bucatini to cook (see pages 50–1 for cooking time).

6 Stir the bacon into the sauce. When the pasta is cooked, drain and immediately toss with the cheese. Either toss in some of the sauce or serve it on top.

• Tagliatelle with • Pea and Ham Sauce

Peas and ham may seem an obvious combination, but it is actually one of the best ways of serving ham that I know – and, since you do not need much, one of the most economical.

The sauce is extremely simple and quick. Consistent with the dictum that the simpler the dish, the more the quality of the ingredients counts, use fresh peas if you possibly can, partly because of their firmer texture; similarly, serve with fresh tagliatelle if possible, ideally home-made plain, maize, chilli or garlic and herb. It also makes a considerable difference to the flavour of the dish if you use smoked ham. Serve with extra pecorino cheese. *For* 3.

• INGREDIENTS •

500 g/1 lb 2 oz fresh peas (250 g/9 oz frozen)

200–220 g/7–8 oz onion (1 large or 2 medium to small)

3 cloves garlic

125 g/4½ oz smoked ham

25 g/1 oz pecorino cheese

8–12 basil leaves

Salt

1½ tablespoonsful olive oil

150 ml/¼ pint single cream

Pepper

375 g/13 oz tagliatelle

Tablespoon
Sharp knife
Grater (optional)
Kitchen paper
Saucepan with lid/or plate
Frying-pan
Large saucepan
Spatula
Colander

• METHOD •

1 Shell the peas. Peel and finely chop the onions and garlic; cut the ham into matchsticks. Finely grate the cheese if necessary. Wash the basil leaves and blot them dry on kitchen paper.

2 Just cover the peas with slightly salted water, bring to the boil, and boil 5–8 minutes or until just tender (with frozen ones, follow the instructions on the packet). Drain over a bowl; then return to the saucepan and cover (with a plate if you have no lid).

3 Fry the onion in the oil over low heat, turning often, 8–10 minutes or until soft but not brown. Add the garlic and cook for 5 more minutes, still turning often.

4 Set the water to boil for the pasta while the onion fries. Start cooking the tagliatelle after adding the garlic (see pages 50–1 for cooking time).

5 Stir the ham into the sauce; if the tagliatelle are not quite ready, remove the ham and the peas from the heat.

6 Drain the tagliatelle. Return the ham and the peas to the heat if necessary and, if your ring responds quickly to a change of setting, turn it up slightly. Add the cream, bring to the boil, and cook at a fast simmer ½–1 minute or until the sauce starts to thicken and is slightly reduced. Add the peas, cook for about half a minute, and stir in the cheese. Roughly tear and add the basil leaves. Remove at once from the heat. Toss some or all of the sauce into the pasta and serve immediately.

• NOODLE STIR-FRIES •

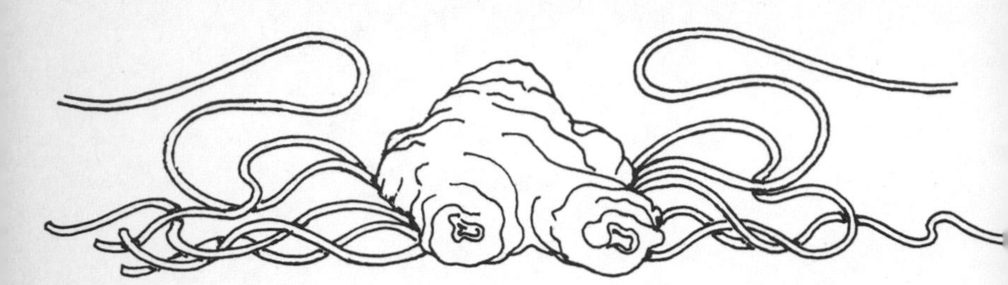

Most readers of this book will need no introduction to stir-frying, but in case anybody is unfamiliar with it, I should explain that it means frying ingredients over a high heat for a very short time, which has the double advantage of saving fuel and ensuring that the food retains as much as possible of its original crispness and flavour. To speed up cooking, everything to be fried is chopped into small pieces; burning is prevented by stirring continuously throughout the cooking time. Full directions are given with each recipe, including details of how to cut up the ingredients. All that need be added here is that it is important not to chop vegetables until just before they are required, since they will otherwise lose much of their vitamin C and may become dried out or wilt.

All the recipes in this chapter are for two or three people, because this quantity is as much as can comfortably be cooked in the usual-sized large wok or frying-pan.

• Tofu and Aubergine • Chow Mein

In this dish, the combination of flavours gives the richness and intensity one normally expects only from meat dishes cooked for a long time with wine. For anyone who thinks tofu is boring, it will be a revelation.

With chow mein (which means fried noodles), the aim is to fry the noodles just enough to crisp and colour them slightly but not so much that they become shrivelled and tough. For best results, use proper chow mein noodles, which are sold at most supermarkets or any Chinese store; otherwise, use ordinary fine or thread noodles. Brown or whole-wheat noodles can be fried very successfully; do not fry spaghetti (which is too thick) or very fine egg vermicelli (the sort packed as birds' nests), which tends to stick together. If these are all you have, simply boil them in the usual way. Having a large frying-pan, preferably non-stick, as well as a wok, makes it easier and quicker to fry the noodles. With only a wok, you will have to part-cook the other ingredients and set them aside while you fry the noodles to ensure that everything is served hot. However, I have given directions for both alternatives.

As Chinese beancurd is seldom available in this country, I have used tofu, which is Japanese.

You can buy oyster sauce at delicatessens or any Chinese store. Vegans should either omit it or use 2 teaspoonsful of medium dry sherry instead.

Use fresh, real spinach, rather than beet spinach or sea-kale beet, which is unsuitable for stir-frying.

You should start to prepare chow mein at least an hour before the meal because the noodles have to be boiled before they are fried and need sufficient time to dry.

The aubergine must also be left for 1/2–1 hour in order for it to sweat. This recipe is enough *for* 2–3.

• INGREDIENTS •

250 g/9 oz chow mein or other fine or thread noodles

Fine salt

375 g/13 oz (1 medium) aubergine

125 g/4 1/2 oz spinach

250 g/9 oz plain tofu

1.5 cm/2/3 inch piece root ginger

2 teaspoonsful cornflour

1 tablespoonful light soy sauce

1 tablespoonful dark soy sauce

2 teaspoonsful oyster sauce

Pepper

1 red pepper

3 cloves garlic

5 tablespoonsful groundnut oil, or 6 if you are using only a wok

Wok
Large, preferably non-stick frying-pan
Tablespoon
Saucepan
Fork or chopsticks
Sieve or colander
Bowl
3 plates
Kitchen paper

• METHOD •

1 Boil the noodles according to the instructions on the packet, separating them as they cook with a fork or chopsticks. Be especially careful not to overcook them. Drain through a sieve or colander and rinse under the cold tap (this is to remove any surplus starch). Leave in the sieve or colander to dry.

2 Wash the aubergine; trim off the stalk end and chop into sticks 1.5–2 cm/2/3–3/4 inch long and 8 mm/1/4 inch wide (cut into 1.5–2 cm slices and cross-chop). Sprinkle with fine salt and leave to sweat in another sieve or on a plate. Rinse under the cold tap (if the noodles are in your only sieve, transfer them to a bowl, use the sieve to rinse the aubergine, and return the noodles to it afterwards). Dry the aubergine on a plate lined with kitchen paper.

3 Pick over the spinach, removing any roots, weeds, or damaged leaves; tear off long stems. Wash, twice if necessary, and cut into wide ribbons. Leave to dry on a second plate lined with kitchen paper. Drain and blot dry the tofu. Dice into sticks about the same size as the aubergine and spread out on a third paper-lined plate. Wash, dry, and quarter the pepper. Remove the core, seeds and inner membrane and any dark spots and chop into strips about 2.5–3 cm/1–1 1/4 inch long and the same width as the tofu and aubergine. Put on the plate with the tofu. Peel and finely slice the garlic and ginger, trimming off any fibrous patches on the ginger.

4 Make the sauce for the chow mein. Thoroughly mix the cornflour with the soy and oyster sauces (or sherry), season generously with salt and pepper, and stir in 3 tablespoonsful water.

5 Check that the tofu and vegetables are dry: blot with more kitchen paper if necessary. Set all the prepared ingredients near the cooker. If your rings are electric and slow to respond to a change of heat, turn one to high and a second to medium.

WITH A FRYING-PAN

1 Heat 3 tablespoonsful of the oil in the frying-pan over high heat until the oil has just begun to smoke. Turn the noodles into it, spread them over the full area of the base, and allow to fry for 30 seconds. Reduce the heat to medium (or change rings), and turn thoroughly. Continue to fry for 3½–4½ minutes, until the noodles are lightly coloured. Do not turn continuously but at frequent intervals: try to ensure that all the strands come into contact with the oil at the bottom of the frying-pan for the same length of time so that they are fried evenly. Remove from the heat. Turn them once.

2 Put the remaining 2 tablespoonsful oil into the wok. Warm over high heat and add the ginger and garlic. Allow to fry for 30 seconds or until just starting to change colour. Add the aubergine and stir. Add the tofu and pepper and stir-fry for 3–4 minutes or until the tofu and aubergine are turning golden. Add the spinach and stir-fry for ½–1 minute, until it starts to crumple. Make a well in the centre and pour in the sauce. Stir to mix it with the other ingredients and allow it to thicken. As soon as it has thickened slightly, remove from the heat.

3 Distribute the noodles into serving bowls and place the stir-fried ingredients with the sauce on top.

WITH A WOK

1 Warm 2 tablespoonsful of oil over high heat. Add the ginger and garlic and allow to colour. Add the aubergines, pepper, and tofu as above and stir-fry for 3 minutes.

2 Transfer the contents of the wok, including oil, to a plate.

3 Wipe the wok to remove any stir-fried fragments and put in 3 tablespoonsful oil. Set over high heat until the oil is just smoking; add and spread out the noodles and allow to fry for

30 seconds. Turn thoroughly and reduce the heat to medium. Continue to fry, turning often, for 4–4½ minutes or until all the noodles are lightly coloured: when turning, stir the strands at the sides into the middle.

4 Remove from the heat and place in the serving-bowls.

5 Put 1 tablespoonful oil into the wok, warm over high heat, and return the tofu and vegetables to it, with any oil. Stir-fry until the tofu and aubergine are golden; add the spinach and stir-fry 30 seconds or until it crumples. Add and mix the sauce as above.

6 Serve on top of the noodles.

• Stir-fried Sweet-and-Sour • Prawns, with Chilli and Lime

The chilli makes the dish piquant rather than hot and because of the proportion of lime the sauce is very slightly sourer than sweet, which accentuates the sweetness of the prawns and red pepper: hence a taster (as opposed to tester's) comment: 'Now this time you have produced a *real* sweet-and-sour.'

You can substitute lemon for lime if necessary, but do not omit the tiny quantity of sherry listed (just two teaspoonsful) if you can possibly help it: its effect on the sauce is almost magical.

The prawns can be served with boiled or fried noodles: fried ones perhaps go with them better but will mean starting preparations over an hour before the meal. For frying, use chow mein or other fine or thread noodles (brown or white) but not spaghetti or very fine vermicelli. I have given two sets of directions for frying the noodles, the first using a frying-pan while the other ingredients are stir-fried in a wok, and the second for cooking with a wok only.

Fresh, i.e. chilled prawns will be juicier and have more flavour than frozen ones; best of all, buy unshelled ones. If, however, you do use frozen ones, remember to allow several hours for them to defrost.

Choose a hard, glossy pepper and small, firm button mushrooms. *For* 2–3.

• INGREDIENTS •

250 g/9 oz chow mein or other fine or thread noodles for frying; any noodles or if necessary spaghetti or vermicelli for boiling

Salt

125 g/4½ oz plain tofu

1 largish red pepper

125 g/4½ oz button mushrooms

50 g/2 oz Kenya or other fine, stringless beans

250 g/9 oz unshelled or 125 g/4½ oz shelled prawns

3 cloves garlic

1.5 cm/2 inch piece root ginger

1½ tablespoonsful (3 dessertspoonsful) freshly squeezed lime or lemon juice (for which 1 lime or ½ lemon is needed)

1 fresh red, yellow, or pod-shaped green chilli

2 teaspoonsful cornflour

2 tablespoonsful white wine vinegar

2 tablespoonsful light soy sauce

2 teaspoonsful medium dry sherry, e.g. Amontillado

90 g/3½ oz soft dark brown sugar

Pinch hot chilli powder

2 tablespoonsful groundnut oil with boiled noodles; 5 with fried noodles, or 6 if they are fried with only a wok

Tablespoon/Teaspoon
Saucepan
Fork or chopsticks
Sieve or colander
2 large plates
2 small plates
Kitchen paper
Cup
Fish-slice
Wok
Large, preferably non-stick frying-pan

• METHOD •

1 If you are planning to fry the noodles, boil them in salted water for the time specified on the packet; separate them with a fork or chopsticks as they cook. Be careful not to overcook. Drain in a sieve or colander, rinse under the cold tap to remove surplus starch, and leave in the sieve or colander to dry for at least an hour.

If you are going to boil the noodles (see pages 50–1 for cooking time), set the water to heat when you have nearly finished preparing the other ingredients. Time them to be ready $6^1/_2$ minutes after you start stir-frying.

2 Drain the tofu and chop into sticks 8 mm/$^1/_4$ inch thick and 1.5–2 cm/$^2/_3$–$^3/_4$ inch long. Spread out on a large plate lined with kitchen paper to dry. Wash, dry, and quarter the pepper. Remove the inner membrane and seeds; chop into strips of about the same length and width as the tofu and place on the paper-lined plate. Trim the mushroom stalks; wash the mushrooms, dry with kitchen paper, and slice finely. Place on a second plate. Top and tail and wash the beans; chop into shortish lengths and put on a small plate lined with kitchen paper. Shell the prawns if necessary (see page 71). Set on a plate. Rinse ready-shelled ones under the cold tap or drain frozen ones; set on a plate lined with kitchen paper to dry. Peel and slice the garlic and ginger, trimming off any fibrous patches on the ginger. Squeeze the lime (or lemon) into a cup. Wash and dry the chilli; pinch off the stalk end, slit, remove the inner membrane and seeds, and dice finely. Do not rub your eyes while handling it and wash your hands directly afterwards.

3 Make the sweet-and-sour sauce. Thoroughly mix the cornflour with the vinegar; stir in the lime juice, soy sauce, sherry, sugar, a little salt, and a pinch of hot chilli powder.

4 Check that the tofu, prawns, and vegetables are dry: blot with kitchen paper if necessary. Set all the prepared ingredients within easy reach of the cooker.

WITH FRIED NOODLES USING A FRYING-PAN

If you have electric rings which do not respond quickly to a change of setting, turn one to high and another to medium. Heat 3 tablespoonsful of oil in the frying-pan over high heat. As soon as the oil starts to smoke, add the noodles; spread them over the whole area of the pan and allow to fry for 30 seconds. Turn thoroughly, lower the heat to medium (or change rings), and fry 3½–4½ minutes, until the noodles are slightly coloured and crisp. Stir at frequent intervals: try to ensure that all the strands in turn come into contact with the oil at the bottom of the pan. Remove from the heat.

After stirring them the first time, warm 2 tablespoonsful of oil over high heat in the wok. Add the garlic and ginger and allow to fry for 25–30 seconds, until just, but only just, beginning to change colour. (As the stir-frying takes 5½–6½ minutes, they may become very brown: keep them well to the sides of the wok.) Add the tofu and pepper and stir-fry for 2½–3 minutes, until the tofu is starting to turn gold. Add the beans and stir-fry for 1 minute; add the mushrooms and stir-fry for 1–2 minutes. Add the prawns and stir. Make a well in the middle of the pan; beat up the sauce quickly with a fork or spoon, and add. Stir it gently with the other ingredients until thickened. Serve on top of the noodles.

WITH FRIED NOODLES USING A WOK

Turn on two electric rings if necessary, as above. Warm 2 tablespoonsful of oil over high heat in the wok, put in the ginger and garlic, and fry 25–30 seconds, until just starting to colour. Add the tofu and pepper and stir-fry 2½–3 minutes; add the beans and stir-fry 1 minute; add the mushrooms and stir briefly. Remove from the heat and transfer the contents of the wok, including the garlic, ginger, and oil, to an empty plate (take off the kitchen paper). Wipe the wok, put in 3 tablespoonsful oil, and set over the heat (still turned up high) until just smoking. Add and spread out the noodles, allow to fry for 30 seconds, and stir thoroughly. Reduce the heat to medium and continue to fry 4–4½ minutes or until the noodles are slightly coloured: turn very frequently, stirring the strands at the sides to the centre. Remove from the heat and distribute into serving-bowls. Put 1 tablespoonful oil into the wok and warm over high heat. Add the tofu and vegetables and stir-fry for 1–2 minutes; add the prawns and sauce as above and serve on top of the noodles.

• Chicken Chow Mein •

As with Chicken Noodle Soup, very swift cooking means that the chicken retains all its original flavour; it is soaked in egg-white and a very little cornflour to give it the lightest crisp coating: further crispness is added by the vegetables.

I suggest using boned chicken breasts, although they are more expensive than leg portions, because they are easier to cut up; however, you can use legs, which are not only cheaper but also tend to have more flavour. For instructions on boning and chopping them, see page 41.

For chow mein, the noodles should be fried just enough to be crisp and slightly coloured, and to taste fried, but not so much that they become hard and shrivelled. If possible, use proper chow mein noodles, which can be bought at Chinese stores and many supermarkets or other shops; otherwise, choose ordinary fine or thread noodles (brown or white). Avoid spaghetti, which is too thick to fry satisfactorily, and very fine vermicelli, which is too thin.

It is easier to fry noodles in a large, preferably non-stick, frying-pan than a wok because the pan has a wider area of flat base; it also enables you to fry the noodles and stir-fry the other ingredients simultaneously. I have, however, given directions for both methods.

Oyster sauce is not sold at most supermarkets but can be bought at delicatessens or any Chinese store.

It is important that the chicken should be really fresh: do not keep it until its sell-by date, but cook it as soon as possible after it is bought.

As the noodles have to be boiled before they are fried, you need to allow at least an hour for them to dry; the courgettes should also be left to sweat for ½–1 hour. *For* 2–3.

• INGREDIENTS •

250 *g*/9 *oz chow mein or other fine or thread noodles*

250 *g*/9 *oz* (3 *small*) *courgettes*

3 *teaspoonsful cornflour*

2 *large or* 3 *smaller sticks celery*

Fine salt

1 free-range egg-white

2 boned free-range chicken breasts

Pepper

1 tablespoonful plus 1 teaspoonful light soy sauce

50 g/2 oz mange-tout peas

3 cloves garlic

1 cm/⅓ inch piece root ginger

2 teaspoonsful oyster sauce

6 tablespoonsful groundnut oil, or 7 if you are using only a wok, plus 1 teaspoonful

Wok
Large, preferably non-stick frying-pan (if possible)
Sharp knife
Fish-slice or perforated spoon
Tablespoon
Teaspoon
3 plates
Saucepan
Fork or chopsticks
Sieve or colander
Kitchen paper
Bowl

• METHOD •

1 Boil the noodles for the length of time directed on the packet, taking particular care not to overcook them; separate them with a fork or chopsticks as they cook. Drain them through a sieve, rinse under the cold tap to remove any surplus starch, and then leave the noodles in the sieve to dry for an hour or more.

2 Wash the courgettes, trim the ends, and chop into sticks about 5 mm/¼ inch thick and 1.5 cm/⅔ inch long (cut into 1.5 cm slices and cross-chop). Sprinkle with fine salt and leave to sweat in a colander or on a plate for 30 minutes–1 hour. Rinse under the cold tap and spread out to dry on a plate lined with kitchen paper.

3 Separate the egg (see page 20). Skin the chicken, if necessary: simply pull the skin sharply from one end. Wash the meat in cold water and dry with kitchen paper. Then lay it out flat and chop into sticks 6 mm/¼ inch wide and 1.5 cm/⅔ inch long.

Spread out the sticks on a plate, season moderately with salt and pepper, and sprinkle with 3 teaspoonsful (1 dessertspoonful) soy sauce; toss to coat them on all sides. Then sprinkle with 1 teaspoonful of cornflour and toss; finally, pour the egg-white over them and toss again. Leave to marinate while you prepare the rest of the ingredients. Wash your hands (as with raw egg, this is always advisable after handling uncooked meat, particularly poultry).

4 Trim the leaf and root ends of the celery and scrape off any brownish streaks. Wash, dry, and slice finely. Wash the peas, trim the ends, and cut into diagonal strips about 8 mm/¼ inch wide: set on a plate lined with kitchen paper to dry. Peel and finely slice the garlic and ginger, discarding any fibrous patches on the ginger.

5 Make the sauce for the chow mein. Mix 2 teaspoonsful cornflour with the remaining 4 teaspoonsful soy sauce; add the oyster sauce and stir in with 5 tablespoonsful water.

6 Add 1 teaspoonful of the oil to the chicken in its marinade and toss to mix. If any of the vegetables are not completely dry, blot with kitchen paper. Set all the prepared ingredients conveniently to hand near the cooker. If you have electric rings which respond slowly to a change of setting, turn one to high another to medium.

WITH A FRYING-PAN

1 Heat 3 tablespoonsful of oil in the frying-pan over high heat until the oil is just starting to smoke. Add the noodles, spread over the whole base of the pan, and leave to fry for 30 seconds. Reduce the heat to medium (or change rings), turn thoroughly, and fry 3½–4½ minutes, until the noodles are lightly coloured and very slightly crisp. Do not stir-fry but turn often: try to ensure that all the strands come into contact with the oil at the bottom of the pan. Remove from the heat. Turn once.

2 Put 2 tablespoonsful oil into the wok. Warm over high heat. Add the ginger and garlic and allow to fry for 30 seconds or until just starting to colour. Add the celery and stir-fry for 30 seconds. Add the courgettes and stir-fry for another 30 seconds; add the peas and stir-fry for 1½–2 minutes. Remove from the heat (including the garlic and ginger) with the fish-slice and transfer to one of the plates. Add another tablespoonful of oil to the wok, warm over high heat, and put in the chicken. Stir-fry for 1½ minutes or until the meat is opaque and beginning to turn gold. Return the vegetables to the pan and stir; make a well in the centre of the ingredients, pour in the sauce, and stir until it has thickened.

3 Serve on top of the noodles.

WITH A WOK

1 Warm 2 tablespoonsful of oil over high heat. Add the ginger and garlic and allow to fry until starting to colour. Add the celery and stir-fry for 30 seconds; then repeat process with the courgettes, for 30 seconds, and peas for 1 minute. Remove the wok from the heat and transfer the contents, including the ginger and garlic, to a second plate.

2 Wipe the pan to remove any stir-fried fragments, add 1 tablespoonful of oil, and stir-fry the chicken for 1½ minutes, as above; remove from the heat and put with the vegetables. Add 3 tablespoonsful of oil to the wok and heat until just smoking. Add and spread out the noodles and allow to fry for 30 seconds. Reduce the heat to medium, turn thoroughly, and fry 4–4½ minutes or until lightly coloured. Turn very frequently, stirring the strands at the sides towards the middle and trying to ensure that they all come into contact with the oil. Remove from the heat and distribute into serving bowls.

3 Put an additional tablespoonful of oil into the wok, warm over high heat, replace the vegetables, and stir-fry 30 seconds–1 minute. Add the chicken and stir for a few seconds. Make a well in the centre of the ingredients, pour in the sauce, and stir until it has thickened. Add to the noodles and serve.

• Boiled Noodles with • Braised Sweet-and-Sour Pork Spare-Ribs and Beansprouts

In this recipe, the pork is cooked very slowly with the sauce for a long time so that the meat is completely impregnated with the flavour and so tender that it is almost falling to pieces. The sauce, which in turn absorbs the juices from the meat, is richer and mellower than its quickly cooked counterpart; it is not thickened but reduced to a syrupy consistency just before serving. It makes an enormous difference to it if you can add sherry, which gives it a depth and interest far removed from mere sweet-and-sour.

To fit easily into a saucepan or casserole and ensure that the meat is covered or partly covered by the sauce during cooking, the spare-ribs should be chopped into two, which will probably mean buying them from a butcher; alternatively, bone them before cooking (simply cut out the bone with a sharp knife).

You can also use pork chops, but try to find those on which some of the lean is interspersed with fat, since a large chunk of lean will be less tender when cooked.

The meat can either be simmered in a covered saucepan on the hob or cooked in a casserole in the oven. The hob is cheaper in terms of fuel but I cannot recommend it without reservation because the smell during cooking is fairly potent: the oven is the more discreet method. Cooking-time is 2½–2¾ hours, but all except the final half hour can be carried out in advance: if the meat is fatty, cooking the previous day is a good idea as the fat will solidify when cold and can be removed.

I suggest serving the dish with boiled rather than fried noodles, partly because reducing the sauce means that frying noodles as well becomes complicated: the beansprouts and other accompanying vegetables are designed to add crispness.

As the rest of the dish has to be served before the sauce is reduced, it is helpful to have a warmed serving-dish: all you need is a deep dish which can be filled with hot water. *For* 3.

• INGREDIENTS •

4 cloves garlic

2.5 cm/1 inch piece root ginger

2.5 cm/1 inch piece cinnamon stick

Bayleaf

500–600 g/1 lb 2 oz—1 lb 6 oz pork spare-ribs or 3 pork chops interlarded with fat

Salt

Pepper

125 g/4 oz soft dark brown sugar

4 tablespoonsful wine vinegar

4 tablespoonsful dark soy sauce

Scant 3 tablespoonsful medium dry sherry, e.g. Amontillado

6 peppercorns

3 tablespoonsful groundnut oil

200 g/6 oz mung beansprouts

125 g/4½ oz button mushrooms

2 largish sticks celery

375 g/13 oz noodles

2 teaspoonsful light soy sauce

Small casserole or medium-sized saucepan with lid
Wok
Fish-slice or perforated spoon
Deep serving-dish
Tablespoon
Sharp knife
Kitchen paper
Bowl (optional)
Colander or sieve
3 plates

• METHOD •

1 Peel and finely slice 3 cloves of garlic, and half the ginger, removing any fibrous patches. Break the cinnamon into 4 or 5 pieces; wash the bayleaf. Wash and dry the meat; unless you are cooking it a day in advance, trim off any excess fat round the edge of chops. Remove the bones from ribs if necessary; bone chops. Season meat lightly with salt and pepper.

2 Make the sweet-and-sour sauce: mix the sugar with the vinegar, soy sauce, sherry, 2 tablespoonsful of water, and a moderate pinch of salt.

3 Put 1 tablespoonful oil into the saucepan, or, if you plan to braise the meat in the oven, the wok. Warm over fairly high heat. Add the garlic and ginger and allow to fry until just starting to colour; add the cinnamon and turn in the oil. Add the meat and fry on both sides for a few seconds, until it has turned pale. Quickly beat up and add the sauce. Add the bayleaf and peppercorns and bring to the boil.

4 If you are cooking the pork on the hob, lower the heat to the gentlest possible simmer: when covered, the surface should move but not bubble. Cover and cook $2^1/_2$–$2^3/_4$ hours or $2^1/_4$ hours if you are preparing it in advance; stir 3 or 4 times during cooking to ensure that all the meat in turn is submerged. (To keep overnight, turn the entire contents of the pan into a bowl, leave to cool, cover, and store in the refrigerator. To finish cooking, skim off the fat, which will have formed a solid layer on the surface, replace in the saucepan, cover, and set over low heat as before for $^1/_4$–$^1/_2$ an hour after it starts to simmer.)

If you are cooking the pork in the oven, remove the wok from the heat as soon as the sauce boils. Set the oven to 150°C, 300°F, Gas Mark 2. Transfer the contents of the wok to the casserole and cook for $2^1/_2$—$2^3/_4$ or $2^1/_4$ hours as above. (If you are preparing the meat in advance, you can leave it in the casserole: simply allow to cool and store in the refrigerator. To finish cooking, return to the oven at the same setting for 45 minutes.)

5 Thoroughly pick over the beansprouts and rinse in a sieve under the cold tap. Shake to remove surplus water and spread out on a plate lined with kitchen paper to dry. Trim the mushroom stalks; wash, dry, and slice the mushrooms and put on another plate. Trim the leaf and root ends of the celery; pare off any brownish streaks, wash, dry, and slice finely; place on a third plate. Peel and finely slice the remaining clove of garlic and the rest of the ginger.

6 Set the water to boil for the noodles; check the cooking instructions on the packet and time them to synchronize with the meat. Start stir-frying the vegetables 4 minutes before they will be ready. Set the prepared ingredients and the light soy sauce conveniently to hand near the cooker; pour hot water into the serving-dish. Put the remaining 2 tablespoonsful of oil into the wok and warm over high heat. Add the garlic and ginger and allow to fry for 30 seconds or until just starting to colour.

Add the beansprouts and stir-fry for $1\frac{1}{2}$ minutes. Add the celery and stir-fry for another $1\frac{1}{2}$ minutes. Add the mushrooms and stir-fry 1 minute. Remove from the heat. Empty the water from the serving-dish and dry it.

7 Drain the noodles and place in the dish. Remove the meat from the heat and arrange on top of the noodles, using the fish-slice or perforated spoon so that the sauce is left behind; if not previously boned, pick out the rib-bones. Replace the wok over high heat and continue to stir-fry $\frac{1}{2}$–1 minute; add the light soy sauce and arrange the vegetables over the meat. Pour the sweet-and-sour sauce into the wok and boil over high heat for 1–2 minutes, until thickened, almost black, and reduced by nearly half. Pour over the vegetables and serve immediately.

• STUFFED PASTA •

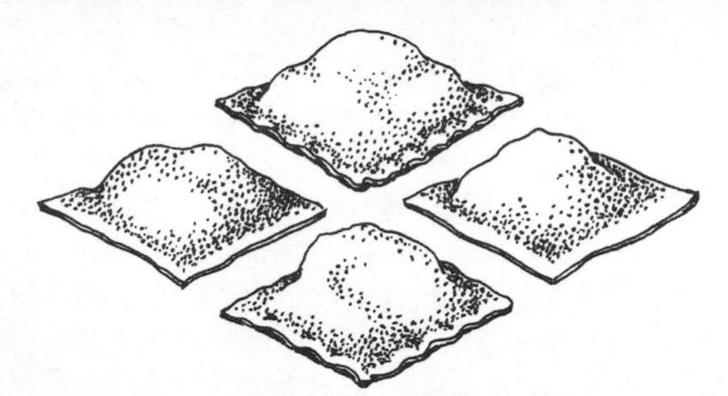

This chapter is complementary to the one on parties, in that stuffed pasta is the obvious choice for entertaining. Not only is it a real luxury, but it has the advantage that both stuffings and sauces can be made ahead of time.

The possibilities for stuffings are almost endless. I can give only a limited number here, but you may like to invent others yourself. If you do, bear in mind that the success of the dish depends not only on the stuffing itself, but on its relation to the sauce that goes with it. You must either ensure that the flavours are equally balanced or design one as the centre of interest and the other as background, as, for instance, with the Cheese and Potato Stuffing for ravioli (see page 104), where the interest is provided by Parsley Pesto or Olive and Tomato Sauce.

It is difficult to be exact about the amount of stuffing needed for both ravioli and cannelloni; with ravioli, the amount of dough wasted because of trimming will vary (with machine-rolled dough, the wastage is far less). There may also be a considerable difference between the quantity needed for hand-rolled and bought cannelloni pipes. As it is less annoying to have too much than too little I have erred on the generous side.

• RAVIOLI •

Making ravioli automatically means making the pasta itself, since the stuffing can only be added while the dough is fresh and you cannot buy fresh dough rolled sufficiently thin. Lasagne sheets are too thick; thinner sheets are not sold, presumably because of the difficulty of preventing them from sticking together. The corollary of this is of course that home-filled ravioli are definitely a bit special: in particular, I suggest them as a first course for a dinner-party, which can be followed by something very simple (see page 146). In view of the time needed for making the dough (about an hour), I have given three very quick fillings which can be prepared between kneading and rolling the dough. However, you can make two of them in advance if you prefer. All the sauces can also be made in advance. *Serves 3–4 as a main course, or 6–8 as a first course.*

• INGREDIENTS •

FOR THE DOUGH

Use the recipe on page 18.

FOR FILLINGS AND SAUCES

See below

Kitchen paper or tea-towel
Teaspoon
Fairly heavy, sharp knife
Sharp pastry-wheel (if you have one)
Pastry-brush (if available)

• METHOD •

1 Mix and knead Rich Egg Pasta dough as on page 18. (As ravioli are supposed to be light and delicate, I recommend white- rather than brown-flour dough; similarly, although you can try using flavourings, the following fillings and sauces are designed and have been tested with unflavoured dough.) Cover and leave to rest. Keep the spare egg-whites.

2 Make the filling (see pages 103–6).

3 Prepare a rolling-out surface and set the egg-whites to hand. Spread the tea-towel or kitchen paper wherever you plan to put the ravioli to dry. Wash your hands. Briefly re-knead the first ball of dough and roll it out as thinly as possible, i.e. to about 36 cm/14 inches in diameter. Use the knife to cut it into two oblongs, making one about 2 cm/3/4 inch longer and wider than the other. Keep the trimmings of dough. (With a machine, the dough will be in strips: this makes no difference except that it will need less trimming.) Place small teaspoonsful of filling at 4 cm/1 1/2 inch intervals on the smaller sheet, leaving a margin of 1 cm/1/3 inch round the edges: you should be able to fit in three rows of 5 or 6. Be tidy: do not spill bits of filling over the rest of the dough. It also helps with cutting to space the blobs of filling symmetrically, making rows downwards as well as across. Paint the pasta, between the blobs of filling, generously with egg-white, which serves as an extremely effective glue (in fact, it is not really necessary, as the pasta will stick using only water, but you might as well take advantage of the egg-whites). If you have no pastry-brush, use your fingers. At this stage, the sheet of dough should look rather like an outsize game of noughts (as opposed to crosses) with the wet strips of egg-white serving to mark the squares. Place the larger oblong of dough on top of the painted one. Press it gently over the lumps of filling to exclude air and more firmly to the dough between. Cut down and across between the lumps of filling to give 15 or 18 squares, using the pastry-wheel if available to give a decorative, serrated edge. Check that each square is stuck all round, trim the edges if necessary, and place a little apart on the tea-towel or kitchen-paper to dry. Fill and cut extra squares from the trimmings of dough.

4 Repeat with the second ball of dough. Before setting the second batch of squares to dry, turn the first over. The only problem with making ravioli is sticking: the moisture in the filling seeps into the dough and if you do not turn them at fairly frequent intervals until they are dry the bottoms will stick to the towel, which may cause them to tear. Fill, stick, and cut the rest of the dough, turning over the completed ravioli when you have finished each sheet. Continue to turn until all the ravioli are dry on both sides.

5 If you did not prepare the sauce in advance, make it now.

6 Boil the ravioli in as much water as possible; unless you have a very large pan, I suggest using two. Salt the water with 1 teaspoonful of salt per litre when it boils; add the ravioli, bring it back to the boil, stir gently, and cook 3 1/2–4 minutes or until the pasta is just tender round the edges. Drain at once and

shake: the irregular contours produced by the filling tend to trap water, making very thorough draining necessary.
7 Toss in some of the sauce and serve the rest on top.

• Clara's Lemon and • Ricotta Stuffing

This is very simple but delicate, refreshing, and novel, since the lemon gives the cheese an unexpected tang.

Serve with Romesco Sauce (see page 106), which can be made the day before; do not, however, make the stuffing in advance or the lemon zest will lose its flavour. *Makes enough to fill Ravioli on page* 100.

• INGREDIENTS •

100 g/3½ oz Parmesan cheese
200 g/7 oz ricotta cheese
Largish lemon (zest only)
Hot chilli powder
Salt

Grater
Teaspoon
Bowl

• METHOD •

1 Grate the Parmesan finely and mix with the ricotta. Wash and dry the lemon. Finely grate the zest (the coloured part of the skin) of half of it and add. Add about 1/6 teaspoonful hot chilli powder; mix thoroughly and add salt to taste.

• CLARA'S CHEESE AND • POTATO STUFFING

Ideally, the potato should be baked, since this will give the stuffing a firmer, more uniform texture; boiling, however, produces a perfectly acceptable result. Similarly, fromage frais is preferable to milk but not essential.

If you plan to bake the potato, you will have to allow about an hour for it to cook: you can either knead the dough and wait for it, or start baking it in advance. Alternatively, you can make the stuffing up to 24 hours in advance. Use a floury potato (or potatoes), e.g. Marfona, Maris Piper, or Kerr's Pink.

Serve with Parsley Pesto (see page 65) or Olive and Tomato Sauce (page 57). *Makes enough to fill Ravioli on page 100.*

• INGREDIENTS •

500 g/1 lb 2 oz floury potato

Salt

50 g/2 oz pecorino cheese

4 teaspoonsful olive oil

1 generous tablespoonful fromage frais or 2½ tablespoonsful milk

Baking sheet or saucepan
Sharp knife
Grater
Fork
Tablespoon

• METHOD •

1 To bake the potato(es), set the oven to 220°C, 425°F, Gas Mark 7. Scrub the potato(es), removing any eyes, place on a small baking-sheet, and cook 50 minutes or until soft all the way through if there are two, 1 hour 5 minutes for one. Skin when cool enough to handle. To boil, peel, cut into pieces, and just cover with slightly salted water. Boil 15–20 minutes or until soft.

2 Finely grate the pecorino if necessary. Mash the potato while still fairly hot. Beat in the other ingredients, adding salt to taste. Allow to cool.

• Spinach Stuffing •

In the interests of flavour, use fresh, real spinach. Serve with Fresh Tomato Sauce (see page 51).

The same quantity of this stuffing, with the same sauce plus cheese sauce on top (see page 114), can also be used for cannelloni.

Both the stuffing and tomato (but not the cheese) sauce can be made a day in advance. *Makes enough to fill Ravioli on page 100.*

• INGREDIENTS •

500 g/1 lb 2 oz spinach

Salt

125 g/4½ oz medium-fat soft cheese

50 g/2 oz pecorino cheese

4 cloves garlic

1 tablespoonful olive oil

Saucepan with a lid
Teaspoon
Tablespoon
Sieve
Sharp knife
Fork
Grater

• METHOD •

1 Pick over the spinach, removing any roots, weeds, or damaged leaves. Put into the saucepan with 1/2 teaspoonful salt and 1 tablespoonful water. Cover and cook over medium heat for 4 minutes. Stir and cook 1–2 minutes more or until the leaves are submerged in liquid and tender. Drain through a sieve. Press out as much water as possible with the back of a spoon and chop finely.
2 Loosen the soft cheese with a fork; finely grate the pecorino if necessary. Peel and finely chop the garlic. Fry the garlic over medium heat in the oil until just starting to change colour. Remove from the heat and thoroughly stir in the spinach, followed by the cheeses.

• CLARA'S ROMESCO SAUCE •

This is a Spanish sauce which, if you use a hot chilli, will be fairly hot, but is otherwise a subtle blend of flavours rather than one which predominates. Although Clara serves it with ravioli, it is also excellent with plain or spinach tagliatelle. Made with only half or a mild (pepper-shaped) green chilli, it also goes particularly well with fish.

As it is baked rather than fried, it needs no attention during cooking and otherwise calls for little more than skinning a pepper and crushing the ingredients at the end, for which Clara uses a blender; it takes only 3 or 4 minutes with a pestle, however, and the result, because it is rougher and nuttier, is in my opinion even better.

I know that a lot of people consider skinning peppers fussy and unnecessary, but as the pepper has to be crushed, it really is necessary here: it is extremely easy and, provided that you char the pepper until it is thoroughly blistered and black, gives it a delicious, charcoal-like taste which will probably persuade you that it is worth it after all. You may also become a convert to roasted garlic, which tastes rich rather than pungent.

To make the sauce as thick and juicy as it should be, you need to use plum tomatoes (see page 53), which have a jammier consistency than ordinary ones: as fresh ones are dear and rather difficult to find, I (for once) recommend using tinned. *For* 4–6.

• INGREDIENTS •

1 head garlic or 10 medium cloves

1 dried or fresh red chilli or, for a milder flavour, 1/2 dried or 1 mild green

1 × 400-g/14 oz tin whole, skinned, plain (not garlic-flavoured) plum tomatoes

50 g/2 oz whole (unskinned) almonds or hazelnuts

1 largish red pepper

1 tablespoonful olive oil, plus a little more if the pepper is baked

Salt

2 teaspoonsful or a little more wine vinegar

Smallish, shallow baking-dish
Small baking-tray or dish (for toasting the almonds)
Another small baking-tray or dish if you have no gas ring (optional)
Sharp knife
Small foodbag
Bowl
Tablespoon
Teaspoon
Pestle and mortar
Tongs or long-handled spoon (optional)

• METHOD •

1 Set the oven to 200°C, 425°F, Gas Mark 7. Pull the cloves from the head of garlic (if necessary). Pick off any bits of dry, outer skin. Wash, but do not peel or chop. Wash and dry the chilli. Trim the stalk end, slit, and remove all the seeds; dice as finely as possible. Do not rub your eyes while chopping it and wash your hands directly afterwards.

2 Pour the tomatoes with their juice into the shallow baking-dish, pinching off the stalk-ends and any stray pieces of skin; stir in the chilli. Add the cloves of garlic: as they will later be taken out and skinned, you can leave them in a clump. Bake for

25–30 minutes or until the juice of the tomatoes is reduced to a thick sauce and the garlic is quite soft.

3 Toast the almonds. Spread over the small baking-tray and bake 8–9 minutes or until the nuts are lightly browned.

4 Char and skin the pepper. You can either bake it in the oven or, if you have a gas ring, set it directly over the flame (this can be fun). Choose the smallest ring, set the flame to medium/low, and put the pepper on its side in the middle. Leave it 1–2 minutes or until the part in contact with the flames is burnt completely black and shiny. If the pepper has a long enough stem, you can turn it with that; otherwise, use tongs or a spoon. Do not pierce it with a toasting-fork or knife, since if it is punctured it will lose its juice and flavour. Turn it so that another section becomes black and charred; repeat at least twice so that the whole surface except where it is indented is blackened. Turn off the ring and as soon as the pepper is cool enough to handle, put it into the foodbag.

To char it in the oven, paint it with oil, set it on a second small baking-dish or the one on which you toasted the almonds, and bake for 40 minutes or until thoroughly blackened. Put it into the foodbag as above.

Twist the top of the bag to seal it and leave for 10–15 minutes. Then pick or peel off the burnt skin, which will come away easily. If the flesh underneath is slightly charred or darkened, so much the better. Cut up the pepper over a bowl, since you will need the juice which will have collected inside. Trim off the stalk end, remove the inner membranes, all the seeds, and any dark spots (as opposed to charred patches) and dice. Put, with the juice, into a mortar.

5 Peel the baked garlic. The skins will be crisp but the garlic inside soft; if it is a little browned, it does not matter. Add with the toasted almonds to the mortar. Crush the pepper, garlic, and almonds to a rough paste.

6 Stir in the tomato and chilli, a generous pinch of salt, the oil, and the vinegar. Mix thoroughly, taste, and add a little more salt and vinegar if necessary.

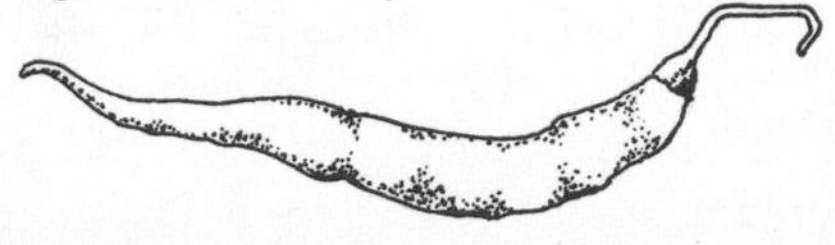

• CANNELLONI •

You are not obliged to make your own dough for cannelloni, since dried pipes can be bought, but the fresh version is infinitely preferable, not only because of the quality of the pasta but the way it is filled: as the filling has to be stuffed into the ready-made pipes, it is very tempting to pack it in tightly, whereas with fresh dough the pasta is rolled round the stuffing, which is therefore relatively loose and makes for a more unified dish. If you use dried pasta, just spoon in the stuffing gently: do not worry if you leave a few unfilled chinks.

The pipes are extremely easy to make: in fact, so far as the pasta itself is concerned, cannelloni is a much softer option than either ribbon pasta or ravioli, partly because it calls for only half as much dough. Against this is the fact that you need not only the stuffing but two sauces, since tomato-based sauces will dry out in the oven unless they are covered, and, besides adding a creamy character to the dish, the cheese sauce gives it a crisp, golden finish.

The cheese sauce must be poured over the dish while it is still warm, but otherwise all the stuffings and sauces given can be made in advance; alternatively, the entire dish can be assembled and kept in the refrigerator for up to twenty-four hours. The following stuffings and sauces have been tested with dough made from plain white flour without flavourings. *Serves* 3–4 (*makes* 16–20 *pipes*).

• INGREDIENTS •

FOR THE DOUGH

Follow the recipe for Rich Egg Pasta on page 18 but use half quantities, i.e.:

125 g/4½ oz flour

¼ teaspoonful salt

1 whole egg, and 1 yolk

FOR THE STUFFINGS AND SAUCES
See below

Fairly heavy, sharp knife
Pastry-brush (if available)
Shallow ovenware dish about 32 cm/13 inches × 22 cm/9 inches

• METHOD •

1 Make Fresh Tomato Sauce (see page 51) or Ragu (page 77). See the following recipes for stuffings. You may prefer to make Olive and Egg Stuffing, which takes 40–45 minutes to cook, before mixing and kneading the dough. (The other fillings can also be made at this stage if you wish.)
2 Mix and knead the dough. With only half quantities, kneading should take less than 10 minutes. Cover and leave to rest. Keep the spare egg-white.
3 Unless you have already done so, make the stuffing.
4 Prepare a rolling-out surface and set the egg-white conveniently to hand. Spread about one third of the tomato sauce or ragu over the bottom of the ovenware dish (this will prevent the pasta from sticking to it). Wash your hands.
5 Re-knead the first ball of dough briefly and roll it out to about 36 cm/14 inches in diameter. Trim the sheet into a square or oblong and cut it into 8–10 squares. (If you are using a machine, the pasta will be in strips: trim it to the length of pipe you want before dividing it into squares.) Place 1 dessertspoonful of stuffing to one side of each piece. Shape the lumps of stuffing into sausages so that the rolls are tidy, and leave a margin of about 8 mm/¼ inch from the edge and ends. Paint the opposite side of the square with egg-white. Roll the filled side over and stick the edge on the egg. Arrange the pipes, with the joined side at the bottom, down the centre of the ovenware dish. Repeat with the second ball of dough: when you cannot fit more pipes down the centre of the dish, set them up each side. They can be placed close enough to touch but not one on top of the other. Distribute the rest of the sauce over the rolls as evenly as you can.
6 Make the Cheese Sauce (see page 114). Allow it to cool for a few minutes and pour it over the dish, making sure that it covers it completely. (Any pasta left exposed will brown in the

oven. Some people, myself included, like the odd edge of oven-crisped pasta, but I leave that to you.) If you are making the dish in advance, allow to cool, cover with foodwrap and store in the refrigerator.

7 To bake, set the oven to 200°C, 400°F, Gas Mark 6 and bake 20–25 minutes or until the top is golden and bubbling. Allow to rest for 4–5 minutes before serving.

• Olive and Egg Stuffing •

The sharpness of the olives contrasts with the egg in much the same way as the saltiness of bacon or anchovies.

Use black olives preserved in brine: pitted ones save time but are less juicy and tend not to have so much flavour as whole ones.

Serve with Fresh Tomato Sauce (see page 51) and Cheese Sauce (page 114): for the tomato sauce, increase the amount of tomatoes from 750 g/1 lb 8 oz to 1 kg/2 lb 4 oz and add just a little extra tomato purée; otherwise, use the quantities listed. *Makes enough to fill Cannelloni* *on page* 109.

• INGREDIENTS •

3 free-range eggs
3 sticks celery (not from the outside)
1 medium onion
2 cloves garlic
500 g/1 lb 2 oz ripe tomatoes
125 g/4½ oz black olives
½ green chilli
2 tablespoonsful olive oil
1 teaspoonful dried oregano
Salt
Pepper
½ teaspoonful soft brown sugar
1½ tablespoonsful tomato purée

Small saucepan
Sharp knife
Frying-pan
Fish-slice or slotted spoon

• METHOD •

1 Hard-boil the eggs: cover with cold water, bring to the boil, and cook 12 minutes. Leave until they are cool enough to handle; then peel and chop.
2 Trim the root and leaf ends of the celery; pare off any discoloured streaks, wash, dry and dice. Peel and finely chop the onion and garlic; skin and chop the tomatoes, discarding the cores. Drain and chop the olives. Wash and dry the chilli (wrap the half you do not need in foodwrap and store in the refrigerator). Pinch off the stalk end if necessary from the piece to be used, remove the inner membrane and all the seeds, and dice as finely as possible. Do not rub your eyes while handling it and wash your hands immediately afterwards.
3 Fry the onion and celery in the oil over low heat, turning often, for 5 minutes; add the garlic and fry for another 5 minutes. Add the oregano and chilli and continue frying, turning constantly, 3–5 minutes or until the celery is soft and the onion soft but not brown. Add the tomatoes; season lightly with salt and moderately with pepper, stir in the sugar, and simmer for 7–10 minutes, pressing the lumps of flesh against the bottom of the pan until dissolved. Add and stir in the olives and purée. Simmer over very low heat 20 minutes: as the sauce is fairly stiff, it will need frequent turning. Remove from the heat and stir in the eggs.

• Spinach and Bacon Stuffing •

An onion and a little streaky bacon make this quite different from the cheese and spinach stuffing already given; it takes a little longer to make but I think is well worth the extra time.

For the sake of flavour, use fresh, real spinach if at all possible; otherwise, choose frozen leaf (rather than chopped).

Serve with Fresh Tomato Sauce (see page 51) and Cheese

Sauce (page 114) as before. For the tomato sauce, use 1 kg/ 2 lb 4 oz tomatoes instead of 750 g/1 lb 8 oz, and just a little extra tomato purée; keep to the quantities listed for the other ingredients. *Makes enough to fill Cannelloni on page* 109.

• INGREDIENTS •

375 g/13 oz spinach

Salt

190 g/6 1/2 oz streaky bacon

1/2 large or 3/4 small red pepper

1 large or 1 1/2 medium onions

4–5 cloves garlic

40 g/1 1/2 oz Parmesan or pecorino cheese

1 1/2 tablespoonsful olive oil

90 g/3 1/2 oz ricotta or other moist, medium-fat soft cheese

Tablespoon
Teaspoon
Sieve
Scissors
Grater
Sharp knife
Frying-pan
Fork
Saucepan with a lid

• METHOD •

1 Pick over the spinach, removing any roots, weeds, or damaged leaves; wash, twice if necessary. Put into the saucepan with 1 tablespoonful water and 1/4 teaspoonful salt, cover, and cook over medium heat for 4 minutes. Stir, and continue to cook (still covered) 1–2 minutes or until the spinach is tender and submerged in liquid. Drain through a sieve and press out as much water as possible. Chop finely.

2 Trim the rind and any bone from the bacon and dice finely (use scissors). Wash, dry, and quarter the pepper. (Wrap the piece you do not need in foodwrap and store in the refrigerator.) Remove the core, seeds, white inner membrane, and any dark spots from the part of the pepper to be used and dice. Peel and finely chop the onion and garlic. Grate the Parmesan or pecorino if necessary.

3 Fry the onion, bacon, and pepper in the oil over low heat, turning often, for 5 minutes; add the garlic and continue to fry, turning constantly, 8–10 minutes or until the onion and pepper are soft but not brown. Remove from the heat. Add and thoroughly stir in the spinach. Stir in the cheeses.

• CHEESE STUFFING WITH RAGU •

Although much the simplest stuffing, I have left this until last because, when partnered with ragu, I think it works best of all: the ragu brings the cheese alive in a quite remarkable way (tomato sauce does not have the same effect).

Use the recipe for Ragu on page 77; top with Cheese Sauce (see below). *Makes enough to fill Cannelloni on page* 109.

• INGREDIENTS •

190 *g*/6½ *oz pecorino cheese*
4 *tablespoonsful milk*
375 *g*/13 *oz medium-fat soft cheese*
Salt
Pepper
Hot chilli powder

Grater
Bowl
Fork

• METHOD •

Finely grate the pecorino if necessary. Mash the milk into the soft cheese. Add the pecorino, a little salt, rather more pepper, and a moderate pinch of hot chilli powder; mix thoroughly.

• CHEESE SAUCE •

This is used not only for Cannelloni but for Pasta Pasties (see opposite) and Lasagne (page 120). It takes only a few minutes to make but must be stirred continuously until it has thickened to ensure that the flour does not form lumps: to shorten the time during which stirring is needed, I have suggested heating the milk first. *Makes enough to go with Cannelloni on page* 109.

• INGREDIENTS •

50 g/2 oz Parmesan or pecorino cheese

50 g/2 oz Gruyère or mild Cheddar cheese (Gruyère is preferable)

450 ml/¾ pint milk

20 g/¾ oz butter

20 g/¾ oz plain white flour

Salt

Pepper

Grater
Small saucepan
Wooden spatula

• METHOD •

Grate the cheeses if necessary. Heat but do not boil the milk in a small saucepan. Melt the butter over low heat; add the flour. Stir until it is completely incorporated; do not, however, let it brown. Add the milk gradually. Add a little salt and rather more pepper and simmer very gently 4–5 minutes, stirring constantly. Remove from the heat and stir in the cheeses.

• Pasta Pasties •

These could be described as either a variant of cannelloni or a larger version of agnolotti, which is small stuffed pasta shaped as half circles. I have suggested making pasties comparable in size to cannelloni pipes but you can cut them smaller if you like: use a tart-sized pastry-cutter or the rim of a glass rather than a tea-cup. If you make them very small, however, stuff them with one of the Spinach Stuffings given earlier (see pages 105 and 112) rather than the Ham or Mushroom fillings that follow, which are designed to be used in larger quantities.

Both the stuffings which follow can be made a day ahead or the entire dish assembled several hours in advance. *For* 3–4.

• INGREDIENTS •

FOR THE DOUGH

Follow the recipe for Rich Egg Pasta on page 18 but use half quantities, i.e.:

125 g/4½ oz flour
1 whole egg
¼ teaspoonful salt
1 yolk

FOR THE FILLINGS

See below

2 large plates
Tea-cup, glass, or round cutter
Shallow ovenware dish about 32 cm/13 inches × 22 cm/9 inches
Fork

• METHOD •

1 Make the Tomato Sauce (see pages 51–5), if you are using it (you can also make the stuffing if you wish).
2 Mix and knead the dough (page 19) using only half quantity. Kneading should take less than 10 minutes. Cover and leave to rest. Keep the spare egg-white.
3 Make the stuffing.
4 Prepare a rolling-out surface and set the egg-white conveniently to hand. Line the plates with kitchen paper. Spread about a third of the tomato sauce over the bottom of the ovenware dish. Wash your hands.
5 Re-knead the first ball of dough briefly and roll it out to a diameter of about 36 cm/14 inches. (If you are using a machine, the procedure is exactly the same.) Use the tea-cup, glass, or cutter to cut it into circles. Place a generous dessertspoonful of filling to one side of each circle, leaving a margin of about 1 cm/⅓ inch. Paint the margin of the filled halves with egg-white. Fold the circles in half, pressing gently over the stuffing to exclude air; seal the edges. Prick with a fork, and place a little apart on a paper-lined plate or, if you are serving tomato sauce, in a slightly overlapping row down the centre of the ovenware dish. Repeat with the second ball of dough. When the centre of the dish is full, place the remaining pasties up the sides.

6 Make the Cheese Sauce (page 114) and allow it to cool for a few minutes. If the pasties are already arranged in the dish, pour it over them; if not, spread about a third of it over the bottom. Set the pasties down the centre and along the sides as above and distribute the rest of the sauce on top, making sure that all the pasta is covered.
7 To bake, set the oven to 200°C, 400°C, Gas Mark 6. Bake 20–25 minutes or until the top is golden and bubbling. Leave for 4–5 minutes before serving.

• Mushroom and Mozzarella • Stuffing

Although this is particularly suitable for pasties, it is also excellent as a stuffing for Cannelloni (see page 109); since the flavour of the mushrooms is more delicate than that of the other cannelloni stuffings I have given, however, I suggest serving it (in either shape of pasta) with Plum Tomato (page 53) or Creamy Tomato (page 53) rather than Fresh Tomato Sauce (page 51), or with only Cheese Sauce (page 114), which brings out the taste of the mushrooms perfectly.

Use large, open mushrooms, which generally have more flavour than button ones. Porcini are not sold in most supermarkets but can be bought at delicatessens or Italian stores.
Makes enough to fill Pasta Pasties *on page* 115.

• INGREDIENTS •

10 g/¼ oz (1 small packet) porcini

375 g/13 oz large mushrooms

3 cloves garlic

Bunch parsley (enough for 3 tablespoonsful when chopped)

200 g/7 oz mozzarella cheese

25 g/1 oz pecorino cheese

1 tablespoonful olive oil

15 g/½ oz butter

Salt

Pepper

15 g/½ oz (1 dessertspoonful) white flour

Frying-pan
2 bowls
Sieve
Kitchen paper
Sharp knife
Grater

• METHOD •

1 Soak the porcini in 150 ml/¼ pint hot (not boiling) water for 15–20 minutes. Drain in a sieve set over a bowl to catch the liquor. Blot dry and dice; keep the liquor. Trim the mushroom stalks; peel, wash, and dry the mushrooms and dice finely. Peel and finely chop the garlic. Trim the ends of the parsley. Wash it, blot dry and chop finely. Thoroughly drain the mozzarella (which is packed in whey to keep it moist); dice. Finely grate the pecorino if necessary.

2 Allow the garlic to fry in the oil and butter over medium to low heat until it is just starting to change colour. Add the mushrooms and porcini, reduce the heat to low, and season moderately with salt and pepper. Fry 12–15 minutes, turning frequently. At first the mushrooms will run juice: continue to fry until it has cooked away. Add and thoroughly stir in the flour: as soon as it is incorporated, add the porcini liquor. Simmer, stirring constantly, until thick. Simmer for another 1–2 minutes and remove from the heat. Leave for a few moments to cool; stir in the cheeses and parsley.

• HAM AND NUTMEG STUFFING •

This is very quick and simple to make and, conveniently so far as time and work are concerned, much better with just Cheese Sauce (see page 114) than with the addition of Tomato Sauce, which kills it. As the ham nevertheless needs some sort of juicy accompaniment, I suggest serving it with green or tomato salad instead.

Use smoked ham and freshly grated nutmeg (the nutmeg is vital). As this stuffing is less suitable than the previous one for cannelloni, I have given only enough for home-made pasties. (It will fill only 9–11 bought cannelloni pipes.) *Makes enough to fill Pasta Pasties on page* 115.

• INGREDIENTS •

250 g/9 oz thinly sliced smoked ham

125 g/4½ oz medium-fat soft cheese

½ nutmeg

Bowl
Fork
Sharp knife
Grater

• METHOD •

Dice the ham as finely as possible, discarding any large pieces of fat. Beat in the cheese with a fork; grate, add, and thoroughly stir in the nutmeg.

• BAKED PASTA DISHES •

Three out of the four recipes in this chapter are for lasagne, which, perhaps even more than cannelloni, is an obvious choice for dinner-parties. The fourth, in contrast, is a convenience dish, in that it is composed entirely of ingredients from the store-cupboard or that you almost certainly have anyway (e.g. onions and celery). Apart from Macaroni Cheese (see page 185), I have not included more baked dishes of this sort, because to be interesting they tend to need a high proportion of flavouring ingredients, which makes them relatively uneconomic. Nor do they have the advantage that they can be made in advance, since the absorbency of the pasta will cause it to take up the liquid: if left to stand for any length of time, the pasta will become swollen and the dish dry.

• LASAGNE •

You can buy lasagne sheets or strips fresh or dried, of which, as always with egg pasta, fresh is preferable (but about three times as expensive). Lasagne, however, is the easiest pasta to make, less because it does not involve drying or stuffing than because it does not need to be rolled quite so thinly.

The quantity of dough required varies slightly according to

thickness and the size and shape of your dish, but 400–440 g/13–16 oz bought fresh pasta will fit a shallow dish about 32 cm/13 inches × 22 cm/9 inches. With hand-rolled home-made dough you will therefore need the full quantity of Rich Egg pasta (see page 18), made with two whole eggs and two yolks. If, however, you are using a hand-operated machine, which does not give the option of a slight variation in thickness, you will need less (the second thinnest ratchet for the rollers is too thick). In this instance, I suggest using half quantity of Plain Egg Pasta, i.e. dough made with two whole eggs.

As with stuffed pasta, the filling must be ready before you roll the dough; but the cheese sauce should not be made until afterwards. The first filling can be made a few hours in advance and the other two the previous day; alternatively, the entire dish can be made with the second and third fillings a day in advance.

Since most of the dried lasagne now available does not need boiling as well as baking, I have assumed that you will use this kind; however, if pre-cooking is needed, boil the strips after preparing the filling, as with rolling fresh dough, since the pasta will stick together if allowed to cool. *For* 5–6.

• INGREDIENTS •

FOR HAND-ROLLED DOUGH

Follow the recipe for Rich Egg Pasta on page 18, but see Step 2 before starting.

FOR MACHINE-ROLLED DOUGH

Use half quantity of Plain Egg Pasta, page 30.

FOR CHEESE SAUCE

Use double quantity of the recipe on page 114, i.e.:

125 *g*/4½ *oz of each kind of cheese*

40 *g*/1½ *oz each butter and flour*

900 *ml*/1½ *pints milk*

FOR THE FILLINGS

See pages 123–7

Extra pecorino or Parmesan for sprinkling

Large tray, dish, or other surface
Greaseproof or kitchen paper
Fairly heavy, sharp knife

Shallow ovenware dish about 32 cm/13 inches long × 22 cm/9 inches wide

• METHOD •

1 Make the filling (see pages 123–7).

2 Mix the dough according to the directions given (page 19) but divide it into 3 balls rather than 4. Knead, cover, and leave to rest. Prepare a rolling-out surface, and line the tray or dish with the grease-proof or kitchen paper on which you will put the rolled-out dough. Wash your hands.

3 Roll the first ball of dough to a diameter of about 38–40 cm/15–16 inches. Trim and cut into broad strips or squares. Lay them slightly apart on the prepared tray. Repeat with the second and third balls of dough. If necessary, you can pile the pasta in layers provided that you put a piece of paper between each layer to prevent it from sticking. (If you are using a machine, simply cut the rolled strips into shorter lengths.) When rolling is finished, cover the top layer of dough with greaseproof paper or foodwrap to prevent it from drying out. Since making the cheese sauce does not take long, this should be unnecessary, but I suggest it as a precaution.

4 Make the Cheese Sauce (page 114). Grate the Parmesan or pecorino if necessary.

5 Spread 1/3 of the filling over the bottom of the ovenware dish. Sprinkle with 1/3 of the grated cheese. Pour rather less than 1/4 of the cheese sauce over the top. Cover with a layer of pasta. Repeat twice, finishing with a layer of pasta: take care to leave enough cheese sauce to coat the top of the dish generously. Pour the rest of it over the top. If you are making the lasagne in advance, allow to become cold, cover, and store in the refrigerator. To bake, set the oven to 200°C, 400°F, Gas Mark 6 and bake for 20–25 minutes or until golden. Leave for 4–5 minutes before serving.

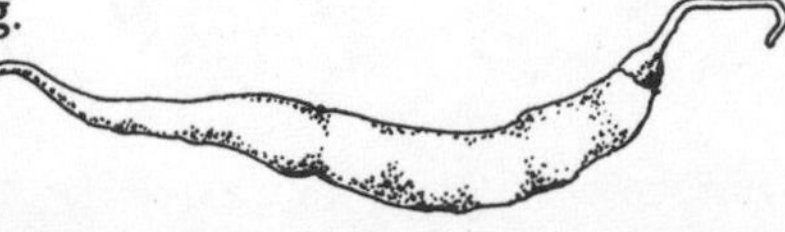

• Courgette and Basil Filling •

I have suggested using about 25 basil leaves for this recipe: if you can manage this quantity, the result is fully worth it, but if you have only a small plant in a pot, just use as many as you (or rather, it) can spare. Take the large lower rather than the upper leaves; do not pick more than half the total number, nor entirely denude any of the stems. If you buy basil, use it as quickly as possible, since it wilts within hours; alternatively, seal it in an airtight bag and store in the salad compartment of the refrigerator, where it should remain fresh at least until the next day.

Small courgettes have a firmer texture and more flavour than large: if they are fresh, they will be hard and glossy.

Allow 30 minutes for them to sweat.

The tomato sauce up to the addition of the basil can be made the day before; the assembled dish can be prepared several hours in advance but preferably not the previous day. If you make the sauce ahead of time, stir the basil into it just before you use it and fry the courgettes before making the cheese sauce.

If you use Parmesan cheese for sprinkling, make sure that it is freshly grated. *For 5–6.*

• INGREDIENTS •

750 g/1 lb 8 oz courgettes

Fine salt

2 largish sticks celery (not from the outside)

1 medium onion

3 cloves garlic

1 kg/2 lb 4 oz ripe tomatoes

About 25 basil leaves

½ green chilli

Pepper

3–4 tablespoonsful olive oil

1 level teaspoonful soft brown sugar

1½ tablespoonsful tomato purée

60 g/just over 2 oz grated Parmesan or pecorino cheese for sprinkling

Sharp knife
Colander
2 large plates
Kitchen paper
Wok or frying-pan
Spatula
Grater
Oven-proof dish

• METHOD •

1 Wash the courgettes, trim the ends, and cut into 1-cm slices. Sprinkle with fine salt and leave to sweat in a colander for 30 minutes. Rinse under the cold tap and leave in the colander to drain.

2 Trim the root and leaf ends of the celery; pare off any brownish streaks, wash, dry, and slice finely. Peel and finely chop the onion and garlic. Skin and chop the tomatoes, throwing away the hard cores. Wash the basil leaves. Wash, dry, and halve the chilli. (Wrap the half which is not needed in foodwrap and store in the refrigerator.) Pinch off the stalk end if necessary from the half to be used, remove the inner membrane and all the seeds, and dice as finely as possible. Do not rub your eyes while handling it and wash your hands directly afterwards.

3 Set two large plates lined with kitchen paper to hand near the cooker. Check that the slices of courgette are dry; blot with kitchen paper if necessary. Season them lightly with salt and moderately with pepper, heat 2 tablespoonsful of the oil over medium heat in a wok or frying-pan, and fry until golden brown on both sides: you will have to do this in two sessions. If the pan becomes dry, add a little extra oil. Transfer the slices when cooked to the paper-lined plates.

4 Wipe the pan, add 1 tablespoonful of oil, and fry the onion and celery over low heat for 5 minutes, stirring often. Add the garlic and fry for another 5 minutes. Add the chilli and fry 3–5 minutes or until the celery is soft and the onion soft but not brown. Add the tomatoes, season with a little salt and slightly more pepper, stir in the sugar, and simmer 7–10 minutes, pressing the lumps of flesh against the bottom of the pan until dissolved. Stir in the tomato purée and simmer 20 minutes.

Tear the basil leaves into three or four pieces and add. Stir and remove from the heat.
5 Grate the Parmesan or pecorino if necessary.
6 Spread a third of the tomato and basil sauce over the bottom of the dish. Distribute a third of the courgette slices over the sauce. Sprinkle with a third of the grated cheese and add slightly less than a quarter of the cheese sauce. Cover with a layer of pasta. Repeat twice, ensuring that you leave enough cheese sauce for a generous coating over the top of the dish. Pour the rest of it over the top layer of pasta. Either allow to cool and cover until needed or heat the oven to 200°C, 400°F, Gas Mark 6 and bake for 20–25 minutes or until golden. Leave to stand for 4–5 minutes before serving.

• FISH FILLING WITH OLIVES •

You might think that the taste of the olives would overwhelm the fish, but in fact it has the opposite effect: the flavour of the fish is enhanced and comes across surprisingly clearly.

For the sake of texture as well as flavour, use fresh rather than frozen fish if possible. The prices of cod and haddock fluctuate: choose whichever is cheaper.

If you are making your own pasta, I suggest Garlic and Herb (page 25), which matches the flavours in the filling.

Pitted olives save time but whole ones are juicier and tend to have more flavour. *For* 5–6.

• INGREDIENTS •

2 *large sticks celery (not from the outside)*

1 *medium onion*

3 *cloves garlic*

500 *g*/1 *lb* 2 *oz cod or haddock*

1–1 1/2 *tablespoonsful olive oil*

1 *rounded teaspoonful dried oregano*

Salt

1 kg/2 lb 4 oz ripe tomatoes
125 g/4½ oz black olives in brine
¾ green chilli
Pepper
1 level teaspoonful soft brown sugar
1½ tablespoonsful tomato purée

Sharp knife
Tablespoon
Teaspoon
Frying-pan

• METHOD •

1 Trim the leaf and root ends of the celery. Wash and dry, pare off any discoloured streaks, and slice finely. Peel and finely chop the onion and garlic. Skin and chop the tomatoes, discarding the hard cores. Drain and chop the olives. Wash, dry, and halve the chilli; pinch off the stalk end, remove the inner membrane and all the seeds, and dice as finely as possible. Do not rub your eyes while handling it and wash your hands directly afterwards. Skin the fish if necessary: pull the skin sharply from the thickest corner. If it sticks, ease it from the flesh with a knife. Wash the flesh in cold water, remove all the bones, and chop into smallish pieces (the size of the pieces is unimportant, since they will flake anyway when cooked).
2 Fry the celery and onion in the oil over low heat, turning often, for 5 minutes; add the garlic and fry for another 5 minutes. Add the chilli and oregano and fry for 3–5 minutes more or until the celery is soft and the onion soft but not brown. Add the tomato; season lightly with salt and moderately with pepper, stir in the sugar, and simmer for 7–10 minutes, pressing the lumps of flesh against the bottom of the pan until liquefied. Stir in the olives and tomato purée and simmer for 20 minutes. Add the fish and simmer for 3–5 minutes or until it separates when prodded with a fork. Remove from the heat.

• Ragu Filling •

Ragu is a traditional northern Italian filling for lasagne, and hard to beat. The addition of red wine is optional but I am more in favour of it here than when ragu is served alone because the amount of cheese sauce with which it is accompanied makes the extra flavour given by the wine more desirable.

The cheese sauce on top of the dish should be sprinkled with a little freshly grated nutmeg before baking.

Ragu goes with spinach pasta (page 26) particularly well, but plain (page 30) or yellow tomato pasta (page 24) are also suitable and easier to make. *For* 5–6.

• INGREDIENTS •

1 large or 2 medium onions

2 sticks celery

250 g/9 oz unsmoked streaky bacon

1 large or 2 small carrots

5–6 cloves garlic

Large sprig rosemary (optional but desirable)

750 g/1 lb 8 oz ripe tomatoes

2 tablespoonsful olive oil

500 g/1 lb 2 oz lean, finely minced beef

Salt

Pepper

150 ml /¼ pint dry red wine (optional)

1½ teaspoonsful soft dark brown sugar

300 ml/½ pint milk plus a little extra

3 tablespoonsful tomato purée

• METHOD •

Follow the method on page 78.

• RIGATONI WITH TUNA FISH •

Apart from celery and onion, you can make this entirely out of the store-cupboard, since it calls not only for tinned tuna fish but hard, i.e. bought pasta, olives, dried oregano, and tinned plum rather than ordinary, fresh tomatoes, which in this instance would not give the sauce the requisite smooth, thick consistency. You will also need stale as opposed to fresh bread for breadcrumbs (fresh bread tends to form doughy lumps when grated).

Use olives preserved in brine and tuna fish in brine rather than sunflower oil.

The fish sauce can be prepared the day before but the pasta should not be added before baking because (as with soups) it will absorb the liquid if the finished dish is left to stand. For 3–4.

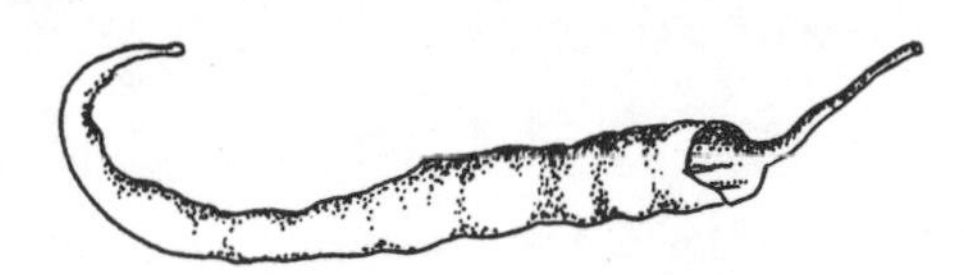

• INGREDIENTS •

3 sticks celery (not from the outside)
1 medium onion
2 cloves garlic
200 g/7 oz black olives
2 × 400-g/14-oz tins unflavoured peeled plum tomatoes
½ green or dried red chilli
2 tablespoonsful olive oil plus a little extra
2 teaspoonsful dried oregano
Salt
Pepper
1 teaspoonful soft brown sugar
2½ tablespoonsful tomato purée
185-g/6½-oz tin tuna fish in brine
100 g/3½ oz stale, preferably brown bread
250 g/9 oz rigatoni

Sharp knife
Tin-opener
Frying-pan
Spatula
Grater
Large saucepan

Tablespoon
Teaspoon
Colander or sieve
Casserole or fairly deep ovenware dish

• METHOD •

1 Trim the leaf and root ends of the celery; pare off any discoloured streaks, wash, dry, and slice finely. Peel and finely chop the onion and garlic. Chop the olives. Chop the tinned tomatoes, removing the stalk ends and any stray pieces of skin; keep all the juice. Wash, dry, and halve the chilli (if green, wrap the piece you do not need in foodwrap and store in the refrigerator; if dried, return to its container, but make sure that it is perfectly dry). Pinch off the stalk end if necessary and remove the inner membrane and seeds from the half of the chilli to be used; dice as finely as possible. Do not rub your eyes while handling it and wash your hands immediately afterwards.

2 Fry the celery and onion in the oil over low heat, turning often, for 5 minutes; add the garlic and fry for another 5 minutes. Add the chilli and oregano and fry, turning frequently, 3–5 minutes or until the celery is soft and the onion soft but not brown. Add the tomatoes, season with a little salt and rather more pepper, stir in the sugar, and simmer 15–20 minutes. Add the purée and olives and simmer another 20 minutes, until the sauce is thick. Drain the tuna fish and stir it in. If you are making the sauce in advance, allow to cool, cover, and store in the refrigerator.

3 Coarsely grate the bread, discarding any hard crusts. Cook the rigatoni in plenty of water for the minimum time directed on the packet; drain, return to saucepan and toss with all but a couple of tablespoonsful of the sauce.

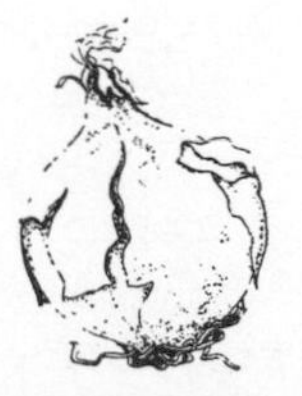

4 Set the oven to 200°C, 400°F, Gas Mark 6. Lightly oil the ovenware dish. Spread the reserved fish sauce over the bottom. Add the tossed pasta, smoothing the top into as flat a surface as possible. Cover with breadcrumbs, making sure that no pieces of pasta are exposed. Drizzle with a little extra oil and bake 15–20 minutes, until the top is lightly browned and crisp. Leave to stand for 4–5 minutes before serving.

• PASTA SALADS •

In a similar way to baked pasta dishes, pasta salads need plenty of flavouring if they are to be interesting. This can be given by the solid ingredients or via the dressing (or both). One of those included here is based on Red Pepper Sauce (see page 66), which has a distinctive, but relatively subtle, flavour; another combines chives, bacon, and pecorino with sour cream; a third is characterized by anchovies and chillies.

• COOKING PASTA FOR SALADS •

For the best result, pasta for salads needs a little more cooking than it does for serving hot. Whereas I have advised boiling it for the minimum time given on the packet for hot dishes, for cold I would suggest one minute longer – i.e. (in most cases) the middle time. Minimum cooking gives hot pasta its characteristic hardness and 'bite', but when pasta is cold this becomes merely toughness. (I do not, however, advise exceeding one minute extra cooking time: cooked for any longer, the pasta will simply be soft and boring.)

It is also a good idea to rinse the pasta briefly under the cold tap after draining. This removes all trace of surplus starch and ensures that it tastes really fresh. I particularly recommend this if it has not been boiled in a very large saucepan.

Unless the recipe calls for tossing with cheese or oil while still hot, the pasta will tend to stick together as it cools: loosen it by tossing from time to time.

• Pear and Pecorino Salad • with Rigatoni

This is based on the combination of pear and a slice of pecorino cheese which I choose whenever I can at Italian restaurants instead of a sweet.

In this recipe, the watercress is used as a herb and chopped very small.

Make sure that the pears are just, but only just ripe. As pears remain at the right stage of ripeness for only about a day, you may have to buy them hard and wait for them to ripen: leave them at room temperature until Williams are yellow and either sort listed below gives slightly to the touch (Conference pears are green or brownish green even when ripe). *For* 3–4.

• INGREDIENTS •

1 *large bunch watercress*

100 *g*/3½ *oz walnuts or walnut pieces*

300 *g*/11 *oz rigatoni*

4 *tablespoonsful olive oil plus a little more*

3–4 *sticks celery*

190 *g*/6½ *oz solid (i.e. ungrated) pecorino cheese*

1 *tablespoonful white wine vinegar*

Salt

Pepper

2 *Conference or* William *pears*

Sharp knife
Sieve, or plate and kitchen paper
Small baking-tray
Aluminium foil
Large saucepan
Colander

Salad bowl
Small bowl
Fork

• METHOD •

1 Trim the ends of the watercress stalks; wash and leave in a sieve or on a plate lined with kitchen paper to dry.
2 Toast the walnuts. Set the oven to 200°C, 400°F, Gas Mark 6. Line the baking-tray with aluminium foil and bake the nuts for 6–8 minutes or until lightly browned. Allow to cool a little and roughly chop or crush.
3 Cook the rigatoni until just tender (see pages 50–1). Drain and rinse; when dry, toss with a very little oil.
4 Trim the leaf and root ends of the celery. Remove any discoloured patches; wash and dry. Dice into 5-mm/¼-inch squares. Put into the salad bowl. Chop the watercress into pieces of about the same size; add. Cut the pecorino as neatly as possible into thinnish strips about 2-cm/¾-inch long and 1-cm/⅓-inch wide (as it is hard and dry, it is difficult to chop tidily). Add to the salad bowl with the pasta.
5 Thoroughly beat together 4 tablespoonsful of oil, the vinegar, and a fairly generous seasoning of salt and pepper. Add and thoroughly toss with the salad. Peel, quarter, core, and cut the pears into 1½-cm/½-inch squares. Toss gently into the salad with the nuts. Serve at once.

• Fish and Farfalle Salad • with Red Pepper Sauce

Although this is not as cheap as one might like, it makes the best of a limited quantity of fish. It is almost, if not quite, as good hot as cold; if cold, it makes an excellent party dish.

Use fresh fish if at all possible. The prices of cod and haddock fluctuate: use the cheapest. *For* 3–4.

• INGREDIENTS •

Red Pepper Sauce (see page 66)

375 g/13 oz farfalle

250 g/9 oz cod or haddock

A little oil (optional)

Small saucepan
Sharp knife
Fork
Large saucepan
Colander
Kitchen paper

• METHOD •

1 Make the sauce. While it simmers, skin the fish if necessary: pull the skin sharply from the thickest corner. If it sticks, ease it off with a knife. Wash the fish in cold water and chop into smallish pieces, removing all bones. Add to the sauce when it has simmered for 15 minutes; continue simmering for 3–5 minutes, until the fish flakes when prodded with a fork but is still firm. Allow to cool.

2 Boil the farfalle for the middle time given on the packet or until tender; drain, rinse under running cold water, and leave to become nearly cold. Turn from time to time to prevent it from sticking together. If you wish, toss with a little oil.

3 Toss the pasta with the sauce just before serving.

• TUNA FISH AND CHILLI SALAD • WITH FUSILLI

This is very much a summer dish, since it is clean-flavoured and refreshing, with piquancy rather than heat added by the chilli. It transforms the taste of the tinned fish, which becomes surprisingly like the fresh version.

Use tuna fish tinned in brine rather than oil.

As given, the salad is enough for 2–3; a very good addition, which will make it quite sufficient for 3, is 200–250 g/7–9 oz tinned sweetcorn.

• INGREDIENTS •

340–375 g/11–13 oz ripe tomatoes

1 lemon

1 1/2 tablespoonful olive oil

Salt

Pepper

1 1/2 medium onions

2 large green peppers

3 green or 2 green and 1 fresh red chilli

8 anchovy fillets (1 tin)

300 g/11 oz tuna fish in brine

125 g/4 1/4 oz fusilli

Tablespoon
Sharp knife
Sieve
Fork
Bowl
Large saucepan

• METHOD •

1 Skin, roughly chop, and sieve the tomatoes. (It may seem silly to skin the tomatoes prior to sieving, but you will otherwise find that they are very difficult to liquefy.) You should be able to purée all but about a dessertspoonful of the flesh. Squeeze the lemon and add 3 tablespoons of the juice, the oil and a moderate seasoning of salt and pepper.

2 Peel and finely chop the onions; add to the purée. Wash, quarter, and core the peppers; remove the white inner membrane and all the seeds and dice into squares about the size of peas. Add to the onions. Wash, dry, and halve the chillies. Remove the stalk ends, seeds, and inner membranes and dice very finely; add. Do not touch your eyes while handling and then make sure you wash your hands afterwards. Drain the oil from the anchovies and dice finely; thoroughly drain the tuna fish and mash. Add both to the salad.

3 Boil the pasta for the middle time directed on the packet or until tender. Drain and immediately rinse under the cold tap. Shake to remove surplus moisture and allow to cool, turning occasionally. Do not add the other ingredients until just before serving.

• Chive and Bacon Salad • with Pasta Shells

The attraction of this salad lies in the contrast of texture and flavour given by the chives and bacon against the pasta and the slight tartness of a sour cream dressing. I have suggested baking rather than frying the bacon because it gives a juicier, more evenly cooked result. *For* 2.

• INGREDIENTS •

60 *g/generous* 2 *oz pecorino cheese*
250 *g/*9 *oz pasta shells*
250 *g/*9 *oz smoked streaky bacon*
Bunch of chives (enough for 2 *tablespoonsful when chopped)*
2 *sticks celery*
1 *carton (*142 *ml/*1/4 *pint) sour cream*
Salt
Pepper

Grater
Large saucepan
Colander or sieve
Scissors
Kitchen paper
Sharp knife
Baking-tray
Aluminium foil

• METHOD •

1 Grate the pecorino if necessary. Cook the pasta shells (see pages 50–1) until just tender. Drain and toss with half the grated cheese; leave to cool.

2 Set the oven to 200°C, 400°F, Gas Mark 6. Trim the rind from the bacon, remove any bone if necessary, and dice into 1-cm/1/3-inch squares (use scissors). Line the baking-tray with aluminium foil, spread the bacon squares over it in a single layer, and bake 8–10 minutes or until crisp but still juicy.

3 If the chives were bought, pick them over, removing any wilted leaves; trim the ends and wash and blot dry. If you pick your own, simply rinse and dry them. Chop very finely. Remove the leaf and root ends from the celery and pare off any discoloured streaks; wash, dry, and cut into 1-cm/1/3-inch dice.

4 Mix the rest of the cheese into the cream with a generous seasoning of salt and pepper. Toss the chives, celery, and dressing with the pasta just before serving. Add the bacon. Taste the salad, and add a little more seasoning if necessary.

• PARTIES AND • DINNER-PARTIES

The contents of this chapter have been controversial, since many people have argued, with perfect justification, that a book on pasta and noodles should include only pasta/noodle recipes. However, I maintain that if people give dinner-parties and want to serve several courses, a few ideas and recipes for dishes to go with pasta (rather than additional pasta dishes) might be helpful.

For a dinner-party centred on pasta, I suggest serving ravioli, cannelloni or lasagne. In Italy, pasta customarily precedes a meat dish: whether the pasta or meat counts as the main course is unimportant. The recipes I have given for cannelloni and lasagne (see pages 109 and 120) are very definitely main-course dishes, after which you will need no more than a salad. The recipes for ravioli, however, could very well be succeeded by, for instance, Chicken Cooked in Milk (page 146), which I suggest because it is simple but at the same time a bit different, and provides a complete contrast in flavour to all the ravioli recipes. The authentic type of first course to serve before cannelloni or lasagne is *antipasti* ('before pasta'), which are small cold dishes. There are numerous possibilities, but the one I especially recommend – because it is relatively inexpensive and (again) a little different – is crostini, which are pieces of crisp bread covered with various items, in this case a selection of baked or grilled vegetables.

The only possible vegetable dish to serve with, or rather after, pasta is salad. Salad greens tend to be expensive, particularly endive, batavia and red lettuce, which go with pasta especially well – although, if only because they are bigger than the standard round British lettuce, these are often better value than they seem. However, besides lettuces and other conventional salad ingredients, you can use baby spinach leaves, coarsely grated carrots and celeriac (these are a good idea in winter), or cooked beans or cauliflower. Whichever you choose, keep the salad simple. You could add finely sliced green or red pepper, baby turnips or radishes to a salad of lettuce, but the only essential is the dressing. The custom in Italy is to add the ingredients for the dressing separately to the salad, but it is probably more prudent to mix them in the right proportions first. For a classic French dressing, beat 1 tablespoonful of wine vinegar into 4 tablespoonsful of olive oil, with a fair seasoning of salt and a little pepper. Make sure that salad leaves are dry before adding it. Do not dress the salad in advance, but toss it with the dressing just before the meal.

The obvious sweet to serve after pasta is ice cream, but Michael's Orange Salad (see page 155) is equally refreshing. Alternatively, try the Lemon Pudding on page 156, which is very like a soufflé. Or, if you want a dish that looks impressive, make the Strawberry Tart (page 148).

The custom in China is to serve a number of different dishes, all of which are cooked separately. Similarly, Kumud Shah described to me a dinner-party given by one of her friends at which the host, instead of offering his guests a cooked meal, invited them to choose from various raw ingredients and then cooked each person's selection individually. For more than two or three people, even the composite dishes I have already given in the chapter on noodle stir-fries will have to be cooked in more than one session. Either of the chow meins or Stir-fried Sweet-and-Sour Prawns with Chilli and Lime (page 88) (which I particularly recommend) would be suitable for a party. If you want to add an extra dish, serve stir-fried French or Kenyan beans with the Tofu and Aubergine Chow Mein (page 84), cauliflower and cashew nuts with Chicken Chow Mein (page 92) and stir-fried celery with the Sweet-and-Sour Prawns (page 88).

As the usual rather uninspired selection offered in Chinese

restaurants suggests, sweet dishes are not a traditional part of Chinese meals. Again, however, you might serve Orange Salad, perhaps flavoured with lime rather than lemon, or Mango and Kiwi Fruit Salad (page 150). Other possibilities are a spiced rice pudding – or, if you do not mind the idea of a second course of noodles, the Spiced Vermicelli Pudding on page 152, which I have included, with another sweet dish made from vermicelli, as an example of a number of puddings that can be made with pasta and noodles, but for which I have not had room to give recipes.

• David Eyre's Crostini •

David Eyre is an increasingly prominent chef, whose cooking has become so popular that he refuses to let me name the place where he cooks, because he says that one single extra customer will probably cause him to close down through overwork. However, one of the dishes for which the customers come flocking is his crostini, a large plate of which many of them find sufficient for a whole lunch. As made by him, they are fairly large: I would say that four each is plenty for a first course. But if you serve more, then a pasta dish to follow that would otherwise serve only four or five might stretch to six or seven.

Basically, crostini are simply vegetables on crisped bread. Their special quality lies in the way that the vegetables are prepared so as to intensify or add interest to their flavour and make them taste as if they were charcoal-grilled. Also, their liquid content is reduced, so that the dish can be made in advance without the bread underneath becoming soggy.

I have given in effect five recipes – one for the bread and four others for different vegetables, namely aubergines, tomatoes, onions and peppers. You can of course serve only two or three if you prefer, but if you make them all, prepare the vegetables in the order in which the recipes are given, since the aubergine has to be left to sweat and the tomatoes to drain. If you want to grill the aubergine and do not have a separate grill, it must be cooked before (or after) the other vegetables.

Since all the vegetables are excellent on their own, as well as on bread, you could serve them not as crostini but simply as antipasti, accompanied by fresh bread and perhaps a plate of olives (unless the next course is Cannelloni with Olive and Egg Stuffing, see page 111).

BREAD

The kind of bread you use is important: it should be solid and close-textured, without holes, and preferably rather stale, partly because fresh bread is difficult to cut tidily. Milk bread or a type of Italian bread called *Pugliese* are suitable, if you can find them. Avoid the more popular kind of Italian bread, *ciabatta*, because it is full of holes, and also French bread, which is too light and dry. *For 24 crostini.*

• INGREDIENTS •

About 500 g/1 lb 2 oz (1 loaf) slightly stale bread

Sea salt

About 6 tablespoonsful olive oil

Baking-tray
Cooking-foil

• METHOD •

1 Set the oven to 150°C, 300°F, Gas Mark 2. Line the baking-tray with cooking-foil. Cut the bread into slices 1 cm/$^{1}/_{3}$ inch thick; remove the crusts and trim into oblongs about 4–5 cm/ 1$^{2}/_{3}$–2 inches wide and 7–8 cm/about 3 inches long.

2 Put on to the baking-tray and bake for 6–12 minutes or until the upper surface is hard and crisp but not brown (the baking time varies according to the freshness and type of bread). Turn and bake until the second side is crisp. Before adding the vegetables, sprinkle each piece with just a little salt and drizzle with about $^{1}/_{4}$ tablespoonful of oil (i.e. 1 tablespoonful per 4 pieces).

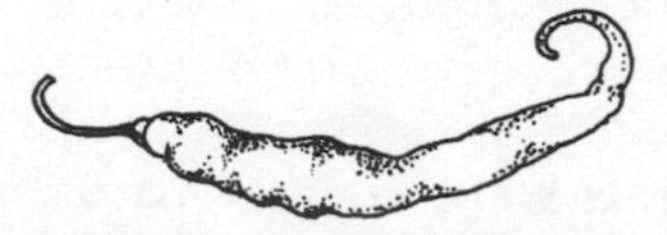

AUBERGINE

Aubergines are very absorbent and, if fried in slices in the conventional way, will soak up large quantities of oil. I have avoided this in the other recipes in this book by chopping them into matchsticks and stir-frying them. David, however, has another method, which is to squeeze all, or as much as possible, of the moisture out of them before cooking. For crostini, he then dry-fries the aubergines on a griddle and moistens them with a little oil afterwards. I have tried dry-frying them in an ordinary non-stick pan and find that it works admirably. However, you may prefer to grill them, which does not produce quite the same result but is satisfactory. The aubergine should be hard and glossy: if it is spongy, it is stale. allow at least half an hour for it to sweat. *For 5–6 crostini.*

• INGREDIENTS •

375 g/13 oz (1 medium) aubergine

Salt, some of which should be finely ground

Small bunch parsley (enough for 1 tablespoonful when chopped)

1 medium clove garlic

5–6 prepared pieces of bread

Pepper

1 1/2–2 tablespoonsful olive oil

1/2 lemon

Sharp knife
Sieve or colander
Grill-pan, or non-stick wok, or frying-pan

• METHOD •

1 Wash the aubergine, trim the ends and cut into slices 1 cm/1/3 inch thick. Sprinkle with fine salt and place in a sieve or colander to sweat for 1/2–1 hour. Rinse under the cold tap and leave in the sieve to drain.

2 Trim the bottoms of the parsley stalks. Wash the parsley and leave to drain either in a sieve or on a plate lined with kitchen paper. Peel and very finely chop the garlic.

3 Fold each sweated and rinsed slice of aubergine into a roll in the palm of your hand and squeeze out as much moisture as possible. If you are using the grill, heat it to medium and grill for 5–7 minutes or until an uneven light brown on the first side (the slices will not colour evenly). Turn and grill to a light brown on the second side. If you are dry-frying the aubergines, put them into a non-stick pan over a moderate to high heat until light brown on each side.

4 Place 2 slices on each piece of bread. Sprinkle with just a little of the chopped garlic and a generous seasoning of pepper. Drizzle about a teaspoonful or a little more oil over each crostini, top with parsley, and add a few drops of lemon juice. Serve when needed.

TOMATOES

If possible, use big, so-called 'beef' tomatoes. If you can only find the ordinary kind, choose large ones. With either, you will be amazed at the concentration of flavour achieved by baking in this recipe. It is a difficult choice to make, but I think that tomatoes make the best crostini of all. Allow 1/2–1 hour for them to drain. *For 6 crostini.*

• INGREDIENTS •

3 beef or 6 ordinary tomatoes
Salt
Pepper
About 2/3 teaspoonful caster sugar
1 teaspoonful dried oregano
A very little oil
6 prepared pieces of bread

Sharp knife
Baking-sheet
Cooking-foil

• METHOD •

1 Peel the tomatoes and slice in half lengthwise (i.e., through the stalk end). Cut out the hard core behind the stalk. To reduce moisture content, pick out the seed pockets of beef tomatoes (but not of ordinary ones). Sprinkle the halves with a moderate seasoning of salt and pepper, the sugar and the oregano; drizzle each with a very little oil. Turn cutside-down to drain for 1/2–1 hour.

2 Set the oven to 200°C, 400°F, Gas Mark 6. Line the baking-sheet with cooking-foil (do not oil it). Place the drained tomatoes on it cutside-up and bake for 35–45 minutes, or until partly blackened and charred for ordinary tomatoes, or for 45–55 minutes for beef ones. Leave on the cooking-foil for 1/2–1 hour (until the liquid seeps through the bottoms and loosens them, they will be stuck to it). Place 1 half of the beef tomatoes or 2 halves of the ordinary tomatoes on each prepared piece of bread.

ONIONS

David uses red onions, but ordinary ones are perfectly satisfactory. Cooked like this, they are almost – if not quite – as good as the tomatoes (they are also much cheaper). *For 6 crostini.*

• INGREDIENTS •

3 medium onions

2 cloves garlic

1 teaspoonful dried oregano

1 tablespoonful oil

1 tablespoonful red wine vinegar

1 teaspoonful caster sugar

Small bunch parsley (enough for 1 tablespoonful when chopped)

6 prepared pieces of bread

Sharp knife
Wok or frying-pan
Cooking-foil

• METHOD •

1 Set the oven to 200°C, 400°F, Gas Mark 6. Cut the onions in half lengthwise (i.e., through the root). Nick out the stalk end, but not so deeply that the halves fall to pieces; peel. Peel and finely chop the garlic. Put the onions, garlic and oregano into a wok or frying-pan with the oil, season lightly with salt, and set over a medium heat until the garlic just starts to change colour. Turn the onions constantly but gently, since it is desirable that the halves should not disintegrate. Add the vinegar, stir in the sugar and remove from the heat.

2 As soon as the onions are cool enough to handle, rejoin the halves and wrap each reconstituted onion in cooking-foil, adding an equal amount of the cooking-liquor to each one. Bake for 1 hour. Allow to cool.

3 Trim the ends of the parsley stems. Wash the parsley and either dry in a sieve or blot with kitchen-paper. Chop finely. Arrange a half onion on each prepared piece of bread and strew generously with parsley.

PEPPERS

The baked peppers taste sweet, rich and creamy, needing no embellishment at all. When prepared, they look rather like thick slices of very dark-red smoked salmon. Crostini made with them are relatively expensive, since you need half a pepper for each; however, the peppers can be small. They should be hard and glossy, without wrinkles or dark spots. *For 6 crostini.*

• INGREDIENTS •

3 small red peppers

Salt

A very little oil

6 prepared pieces of bread

Large foodbag
Baking-sheet
Cooking-foil

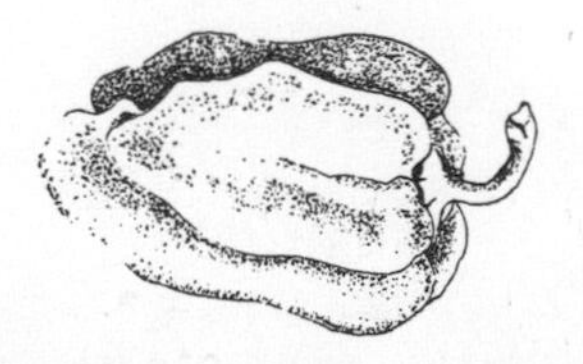

• METHOD •

1 Skin the peppers either by roasting them in the oven or by setting them on a naked gas flame until black and blistered all over. As soon as they are cool enough to handle, put into a large foodbag, seal, and leave for 10–15 minutes. Skin carefully, removing any charred fragments. For further details of how to skin peppers, see page 106.

2 Set the oven to 200°C, 400°F, Gas Mark 6. Line the baking-tray with cooking-foil. Paint the peppers with oil (leave them whole) and bake for 20–25 minutes or until slightly darkened and charred. Allow to rest on the cooking-foil for 1/2–1 hour (if you try to remove them immediately, you will find that they are stuck). Halve them, shaking out the liquid inside, and remove the core, seeds and inner membrane. Season lightly with salt and place outer side up on the prepared pieces of bread.

• CHICKEN COOKED IN MILK •

The idea for this came from Elizabeth David's *Italian Food* (Penguin, 1954 ed.), in which she gives a recipe for pork braised in milk and subsequently observes that chicken can be cooked in the same way. As far as I am concerned, the following (which is not quite the same as her recipe) is addictive, rather like the Strawberry Tart on page 148: once you have tried it, you will make it again and again. The taste of the chicken is wonderfully enhanced and enriched by the milk, and, as the dish is cooked covered, the thyme and other flavourings also come across strongly. It is the perfect dish to follow home-made ravioli, not only because it is a complete contrast, but because it is as easy as possible to prepare. Virtually all you have to do is to chop an onion, garlic and a little ham and wait for it to cook. It needs no accompaniment except a few scrubbed, boiled new potatoes to mop up the sauce.

The chicken should be as fresh as possible. It will take 1½–1¾ hours to cook. For 4–6.

• INGREDIENTS •

1 medium onion

3 cloves garlic

1 bayleaf

4 or 5 good-sized sprigs thyme

50 g/2 oz sliced ham

1 free-range chicken weighing 1.75–2 kg/4–4½ lb

Sea salt

20 g/¾ oz butter

1 tablespoonful oil

4 or 5 peppercorns

900 ml/1½ pints milk

Sharp knife
Large wok with a lid, or iron-bottomed casserole, or covered saucepan large enough to contain the chicken
Tablespoon
Carving-knife for serving

• METHOD •

1 Peel and finely chop the onion and garlic. Wash the bayleaf and thyme; dice the ham. Wash the chicken thoroughly inside and out in cold water, then wipe dry. Rub with a fairly generous seasoning of sea salt.

2 Put the butter and oil into the wok, casserole or saucepan over a moderate heat; add the onion and fry for ½–1 minute, until it begins to soften. Add the garlic and ham and fry until the garlic is just beginning to colour. Put in the chicken, breast upwards, and fry until the underside is lightly browned. Turn on its side (you will need two implements) and fry until the side is lightly browned. Then lightly brown the breast and second side. Turn the chicken back breast upwards, as it was put in, add the bayleaf, thyme and peppercorns, and pour in the milk. Bring to the boil, lower the heat to a simmer, and cook almost covered (put on the lid, but leave a tablespoon in it with the handle sticking out so that the lid is not closed; the spoon will be needed for basting later). Leave to simmer for 1 hour.

3 After an hour, the milk will have formed a golden skin. Stir it in and baste the chicken. Cover and simmer for another 30 minutes, basting every now and again. Test the chicken by inserting a knife as far as you can into the deepest part of the breast. When the chicken is cooked through, the meat will be tender and no liquid will emerge. If the sauce is already thick and brownish, serve straight away. If there is still quite a lot of milk left, turn up the heat to medium and reduce, with the pan uncovered, until it is a thick sauce. The sauce, I have to confess, is rather messy-looking, but this is more than made up for by the taste. Transfer the chicken to a serving-plate and carve; serve the sauce separately.

4 To carve the chicken, cut off the legs, separating the joint at the bottom by twisting sharply. If you wish, divide the legs into two by cutting through the knee joint. Slice the breast diagonally from the central breastbone.

• Strawberry Tart •

Until I decided to include this tart here, I had not made it for a long time. I am now reminded why – when I did make it, for a very long time I seldom made any other pudding during the strawberry season. With its lemon-flavoured glaze, it is one of the very best ways of bringing out the flavour of strawberries – and making just 375 g/13 oz go a long way.

Although it looks very beautiful and accomplished, it is deceptively easy to make, and fairly quick. The pastry can be made the day before (wrap in foodwrap and store in the refrigerator); alternatively, if you have room in the refrigerator for the tart-tin, you can roll it out and line the tin in advance.

For pastry, the opposite principle to that for making pasta applies: in order to achieve a soft, melting texture, you should work it as little as possible. Rub the fat gently into the flour and roll out the dough quickly.

As with pasta, allow half an hour for the dough to rest. *For 6.*

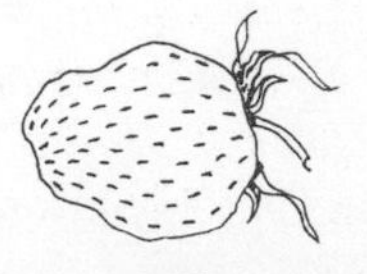

• INGREDIENTS •

PASTRY

50 g/2 oz butter straight from the refrigerator and
25 g/1 oz lard straight from the refrigerator or
90 g/3½ oz chilled butter

190 g/6½ oz plain white flour, plus extra for sprinkling
Salt
About 2 tablespoonsful very cold water

FILLING

375 g/13 oz strawberries
3 size-2 egg-yolks
75 g/3 oz caster sugar
25 g/1 oz flour
300 ml/½ pint milk
½ lemon
190 g/6½ oz (half a 375-g pot) redcurrant jelly

Rolling-pin (long or otherwise)
Board or surface for rolling out
22 cm/8½ inch tart-tin
Cooking-foil
2 bowls
Egg-whisk
Saucepan

• METHOD •

1 Make the pastry. Chop the fat(s) into small squares. Mix the flour with a pinch of salt: if the butter is heavily salted, you will need very little. Rub the fat into the flour with your fingertips until the mixture resembles fine breadcrumbs. Make a well in the middle and add 1½ tablespoonsful of cold water. Form the dough into a ball: not quite all the flour will be taken up. Gradually add as much water as is needed to incorporate the rest, but not more, since if the dough is too wet the pastry will be tough. Wrap it in foodwrap without further handling and leave to rest in the refrigerator for half an hour.

2 Pick over, wash and hull the strawberries; cut off any soft patches. Lay on a plate lined with kitchen paper to dry.

3 Roll out the pastry. Dust the rolling-pin and rolling-out surface with flour. Lightly grease the tart-tin and place conveniently to hand. Unless you are making the pastry in advance, set the oven to 200°C, 400°F, Gas Mark 6. Quickly roll out the dough to a thickness of about 5 mm/less than 1/4 inch. If it breaks, gather it up, re-form it into a ball, sprinkle more flour over the pin and board, and re-roll. Lift it carefully and place it over the tin: press it gently into the edges at the bottom and trim off the surplus. If there are any cracks, use the surplus to patch them: damp the underside with cold water to make it stick. Cover the tart-tin, including the sides and top, with cooking-foil; press it down closely to the pastry. Check that the oven is fully heated and bake for 10 minutes. Remove the foil and bake for a further 15–20 minutes, until the pastry is lightly coloured. Leave to cool.

4 Make the pastry cream. Separate the eggs: wash them (in case bits of shell fall into the contents), crack them sharply in the middle on the edge of a bowl, hold them over the bowl and tip the yolks from one half of the shell to the other, until all the white has fallen out. Empty the yolks into a second bowl. Add the sugar to the yolks and whisk until thoroughly amalgamated. Whisk in the flour by degrees; if the whisk sticks as the mixture becomes stiffer, stir it in with a spoon. Heat but do not boil the milk. Whisk the hot milk gradually into the yolks and sugar. Pour the mixture into the saucepan in which you heated the milk and bring to the boil, stirring continuously (watch carefully, since the whisking will mean that it is already frothy and bubbly). The mixture will thicken considerably. Reduce the heat to a simmer and cook for 3 1/2 minutes; stir continuously. Remove from the heat and allow to cool a little. Spread in an even layer over the pastry base.

5 Arrange the strawberries over the cream; if they are large, cut them in half. Squeeze the lemon. Put the juice and redcurrant jelly into a small saucepan, bring to the boil and boil for 1 1/2 minutes. Allow to cool a little; if the jelly does not thicken as it cools, boil briefly again. It is important that it should set into a firm (but not gluey) glaze over the strawberries. When it starts to set, drizzle it over the top of the tart, making sure that the strawberries are completely covered. If the tart-tin has a movable base, slide the tart from the sides of the tin and set on a plate. Serve at room temperature, with cream if you wish. Finish it off if possible, since it tends to become soggy if kept.

• MANGO AND KIWI FRUIT SALAD •

This is more festive and, mainly because of the mango, rather dearer than Michael's Orange Salad (see page 155) – although you can sometimes buy mangoes for as little as 75p. Take care, however, to choose one at the right stage of ripeness: it should give slightly to the touch but not be very soft (colour is little help, since a ripe mango can be pale yellow or deep red, according to type). The pears and kiwi fruit should also give slightly to the touch but should not be soft. If possible, choose navel oranges. In general, small oranges have more flavour than large. *For* 4–6.

• INGREDIENTS •

2 *oranges*
1 *mango*
2 Williams *or other pears*
2 *kiwi fruit*
1 *lime*
20 *g*/¾ *oz caster sugar*

Small, sharp knife
Serving-bowl

• METHOD •

1 Peel the oranges with the knife, removing all the pith; cut into slices across the middle and halve each slice, removing the tough centres. Put into a serving-bowl.
2 Peel the mango and slice thickly as far as the stone on each side; then cut the flesh from round the stone. Chop the slices into cubes and add to the oranges.
3 Peel, quarter, core and slice the pears. Peel and slice the kiwi fruit, trimming off the stalk end. Add both to the bowl.
4 Squeeze the lime, mix the juice with the sugar and add. Chill the salad for 2–3 hours before serving.

• Spiced Vermicelli Pudding •

Whereas in China cooked sweet dishes are generally treated as snacks rather than forming part of a meal, in India they are not served after the main course but at the same time: this pudding (which is a traditional Indian dish called Beernj) would probably accompany a hot curry, not to be eaten simultaneously but as a contrast directly afterwards.

It is very easy to make and can be served hot or cold: hot, the taste is predominantly rich and fudgy; when cold, the spices are much more in evidence.

The recipe, which was given to me by the cookery demonstrator Kumud Shah, is supposed to include saffron; however, as the cheaper powdered saffron has very little taste and the spice in its whole form (threads) is expensive, I tried it without and found that it was still excellent.

The pudding takes 1 hour to cook. *For* 3–4.

• INGREDIENTS •

100 *g*/3½ *oz vermicelli*
100 *g*/3½ *oz butter*
300 *ml*/½ *pint milk*
300 *ml*/½ *pint water*
2 *saffron threads (optional)*
150 *g*/5 *oz white sugar (caster or granulated)*
50–100 *g*/2–3½ *oz whole almonds*
3 *cardamom pods*

Medium-sized saucepan
Spatula
Baking tray
Pestle and mortar
Bowl

• METHOD •

1 Break the strands of vermicelli into 4. Roughly chop the butter and put it into a medium-sized saucepan. Melt over medium to highish heat, add the vermicelli, and fry, stirring continuously for 3–4 minutes or until the pasta is a rich, even brown. Pour in the milk (stand back, as the mixture may splutter); add the water and saffron, bring to the boil, and simmer for 30 minutes or until all the liquid has been absorbed. Add the sugar and simmer for another 30 minutes or until most of the liquid has again been absorbed, leaving only enough for sauce. When the pudding is ready, the butter should float on top.

2 While the vermicelli mixture simmers, toast the almonds and crush the cardamom. Set the oven to 200°C, 400°F, Gas Mark 6. Bake the almonds for 14–16 minutes or until lightly browned. Allow to cool for a few minutes: chop or lightly crush in a mortar. Break the cardamom pods with a pestle: shake out and crush the seeds, discarding the pods.

3 Stir the cardamom powder into the pudding. Turn into a bowl and scatter the top with almonds. Serve hot or cold alone, as an accompaniment to curry, or with yoghurt or cream.

• Rich Coconut • Fudge Vermicelli

Without the addition of fruit, this is a classic Indian dish: Kumud Shah, however, adds dried figs and apricots, which provide a juicy contrast to the nuts and crisp-fried vermicelli. If served plain, it is something like a very light, much richer, crisper version of muesli: accompany it with a large bowl of thick yoghurt, the tartness of which perfectly offsets its sweetness. Alternatively, you can turn it into a pudding by mixing it with the yoghurt and decorating it with fresh fruit. (It makes it more expensive, but you could serve extra fresh fruit, such as a bunch of grapes, to eat with it.)

Without the fresh fruit, it is astonishingly cheap; it is also one of the quickest and easiest sweets I know, since virtually all you have to do is chop or crush small quantities of fruit and nuts and fry the vermicelli, which takes 4 minutes.

Much as I normally favour fresh ingredients, in this instance it is important to use not only dried fruit to mix with the vermicelli but desiccated rather than freshly grated coconut, since the vermicelli will otherwise become soggy.

For the same reason, do not add yoghurt until just before serving. The dry mixture, however, can be prepared one, or even two, days ahead of time. For 4–6.

• INGREDIENTS •

40 g/1 1/2 oz whole, unskinned almonds

35 g/scant 1 1/2 oz walnuts, hazelnuts, cashew, or pistachio nuts

75 g/3 oz mixed dried apricots and figs (3 figs and 3 or 4 apricots)

100 g/3 1/2 oz fine egg vermicelli

50 g/2 oz desiccated coconut

90 g/3 1/2 oz soft brown sugar

90 g/3 1/2 oz butter, preferably only lightly salted

450 g/1 lb thick plain yoghurt

FOR DECORATION (OPTIONAL)

1 kiwi fruit

25–50 g/1–2 oz grapes

Pestle and mortar
Sharp knife
Saucepan
Wooden spoon
2 bowls

• METHOD •

1 Roughly crush the nuts, leaving a few larger fragments. Wash and thoroughly dry the figs and apricots. Trim the hard tops of the figs and dice both (cut into strips and cross-chop). Separate any pieces of fruit which stick together. If you are using vermicelli sticks, break them into short lengths; if nests, slice them twice horizontally so that they will disintegrate quickly during cooking.

2 Set the crushed nuts, dried fruit, coconut, and sugar within easy reach of the cooker. Roughly chop the butter and put it into a saucepan (in India ghee, or clarified butter, would be used). Melt over low heat. Raise the heat to medium and add the vermicelli. Fry, stirring and chopping continuously to separate the strands and ensure even cooking, for 3½–4 minutes or until a uniform light brown. (The butter will also have turned light brown.) Remove from the heat and immediately stir in the sugar. Then quickly stir in the chopped nuts. Finally thoroughly stir in the dried fruit and coconut. As it is stirred the vermicelli will break into short lengths. Leave to cool. If you have made it in advance, cover when (but not before) it is completely cold and store in the refrigerator.

3 To serve dry, mix again and heap into a bowl, with the yoghurt in another bowl. If you plan to turn it into a pudding, prepare the fruit for decoration. Wash and drain or blot dry the grapes; slice in half and (unless seedless) remove the pips. Peel the kiwi fruit, using a knife if necessary, and slice thinly. Just before serving, mix the vermicelli into the yoghurt and arrange the fruit on top.

• Michael's Orange Salad •

This is light, refreshing, and simple, and altogether the perfect choice of sweet after a main course of either pasta or noodles. You can serve it alone or with Florentines (see page 157) or, which is the option I would choose, serve it alone and follow it with Florentines to accompany coffee.

Oranges present a problem in that many of them are bland and boring and it is difficult to advise on how to select those with flavour. Occasionally you may see blood oranges (very small oranges patched with red) in the shops: if you do, buy them, since they are usually exceptionally tangy and sweet. Rather than partnering them with lemon, as below, do not add anything until you have tasted them, as they may need nothing except the very slightest sprinkling of sugar to encourage the juice to run. The only guide I can give to other oranges is to buy navels if possible and choose small rather than large.

The addition of lemon and lemon peel in the following recipe is designed to give the sharpness that the oranges will probably lack. An alternative is to use limes, which produce a subtler, more interesting result but do not go so well with the Florentines.

Allow 2–3 hours for the juice to run before serving. *For* 4–6.

• INGREDIENTS •

6 oranges, or 8 if very small

1 large lemon or 2 limes

50 g/2 oz caster sugar

Sharp knife
Grater
Salad bowl

• METHOD •

1 Peel the oranges with the knife, trimming off all the white pith. Slice fairly thinly across, discarding the pips; then cut the slices in half through the middle, removing the fibrous centres. Put into the salad bowl.

2 Wash, dry, and finely grate the zest of the lemon or limes (the coloured part of the skin) over the oranges. Squeeze, and stir the sugar into the juice. Pour over the oranges and chill in the refrigerator for 2–3 hours.

• Lemon Pudding •

This is based on a traditional Italian pudding, although the recipe is my own adaptation. If you eat it hot, it is like a sort of soufflé; if cold, it is a cross between a pudding and a cake. I think it is marginally better hot, but it may be more convenient to serve it cold, because you can then bake it in advance.

It takes only 15–20 minutes to make and 25–30 minutes to bake. *For* 4–6.

• INGREDIENTS •

40 g/1 1/2 oz plain white flour

250 g/9 oz ricotta cheese

1 orange (zest only)

150 g/5 oz caster sugar

1 dessertspoonful thick honey

3 size-2 eggs

1 1/2 lemons
40 g/1 1/2 oz butter
1 cm/1/2 inch piece cinnamon stick
75 g/3 oz dried apricots
50 g/2 oz raisins
Salt

Grater
Large bowl
Sharp knife
Soufflé or other ovenware dish about 20 cm/8 inches across and 7 cm/3 inches deep
Egg-whisk

• METHOD •

1 Beat the flour into the cheese. Wash, dry and finely grate in the zest (the coloured part of the skin) of the orange and the whole lemon. Squeeze the lemon plus half of a second; add 4 tablespoonsful of the juice. Melt the butter; allow to cool and add. Pound the cinnamon to a powder and add. Stir in the sugar and honey. Separate the eggs: wash them (in case pieces of shell fall into the whites) and crack sharply in the middle on the edge of a largish bowl; hold over the bowl and tilt the yolks from one half of the shell to the other until all the white has fallen out. Add the yolks to the cheese; stir in thoroughly. Finely dice and add the apricots; separate the raisins if necessary and add.

2 Set the oven to 200°C, 400°F, Gas Mark 6; lightly butter the soufflé dish. Add a small pinch of salt to the egg-whites and whisk until close-textured and stiff enough to hold their shape completely when lifted on the whisk. Fold into the cheese mixture: gently stir in about one-third of the whites at a time with a diagonal, downward motion. Continue to stir gently until the mixture is perfectly smooth.

3 Turn the mixture carefully into the dish and bake for 40 minutes or until well browned and risen like a soufflé. When slightly shaken, the pudding should be quite firm. Serve hot or cold.

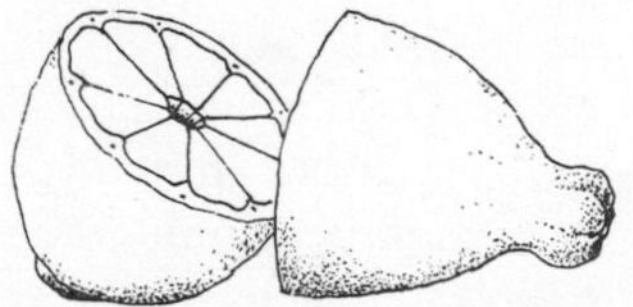

• FLORENTINES •

I admit that these are an extravagance, since they consist chiefly of nuts bound with butter and sugar with no flour or other thickening agent; also, the bottoms are conventionally painted with chocolate, which, as quite a lot is needed, adds considerably to their cost. In fact, however, they are not so expensive as they sound, as only a teaspoonful of the mixture is needed for each one, and the chocolate can be omitted; personally, I prefer them without.

They go particularly well with Orange Salad (see page 155), or can be served instead of a pudding with coffee.

If you do wish to cover the bottoms with chocolate, use plain, preferably bitter cooking chocolate such as Menier Chocolat Pâtissier or Sainsbury's Deluxe Continental Chocolate.

It is important to use ordinary rather than extra thick double cream. *Makes about 36 biscuits.*

• INGREDIENTS •

200 g/7 oz of at least two of the following: almonds, hazelnuts, walnuts, peanuts, pecans

50 g/2 oz raisins

1 orange (zest only)

2-cm/¾-inch piece of cinnamon stick

2 cardamom pods

50 g/2 oz butter

125 g/4½ oz caster sugar

3 tablespoonsful double cream

200 g/7 oz plain, bitter cooking chocolate (optional)

Pestle and mortar
Grater
Knife
Small saucepan
Spatula
Table knife
Large baking-tray (preferably about 31 cm/12 inches square)
Aluminium foil

Pudding-basin which will fit into a saucepan (if you are using chocolate)

• METHOD •

1 Roughly crush the nuts one sort at a time (it is unsatisfactory to crush all of them together because some kinds are harder than others). To vary the texture, leave some fairly large pieces. Separate the raisins if necessary and add. Wash and dry the orange, finely grate the zest (the orange part of the skin) and add. (Eat the fruit on the same day, as it will soon go mouldy.) Pound the cinnamon to a powder with a pestle and mortar. Crush the cardamom pods and shake out and crush the seeds; discard the pods. Mix the spices with the nuts.

2 Set the oven to 180°C, 350°F, Gas Mark 4. Chop the butter into pieces and put into a smallish saucepan with the sugar. Set over medium heat, stir until boiling, and boil for 1 minute, stirring continuously. Remove from the heat and immediately stir in the cream. Add and stir in the nuts, raisins, and spices. Leave to cool for a few minutes.

3 Line the baking-tray with the aluminium foil: take care to lay the foil shiny side up. Generously grease the foil with butter. Place teaspoonsful of the mixture very well apart on the tray. It spreads surprisingly: on a 31-cm/12-inch-square tray, you should place only 9, which means that you will have to bake the biscuits in 4 sessions (since they need shaping while they are still hot, however, it is advisable to bake only a few at a time anyway). Bake 6–9 minutes, until they are a rich, medium- as opposed to golden-brown: they may look ready when golden but will not be sufficiently cooked to be crisp. Set a table- or other blunt-ended knife to hand, and as soon as you take them out of the oven use it to close and shape the edges into neat circles. You will only be able to do this while they are still hot – and they cool quickly: if they have hardened before you have finished, return them to the oven for 1/2–1 minute: the heat will re-melt them. Remove the foil from the baking-tray with the biscuits on it, re-line the tray, and repeat the baking and shaping with the rest of the mixture. Leave all the biscuits on their sheets of foil until they are completely cold. Then peel off the foil.

4 If you want to add chocolate, place them upside down. Break up the chocolate and put into the pudding-basin. About one-third fill the saucepan into which it will fit with water. Put the basin into the saucepan and set over medium heat until the chocolate is almost melted. Remove from the heat and stir until smooth. Place a mug of hot water to hand and, using the knife, spread a layer of chocolate over the bottom of each biscuit; if the knife becomes sticky, dip it into the hot water. Make a wavy pattern in the chocolate with a fork. Leave the coated biscuits upside down until the chocolate has set, which will take several hours. When the chocolate is completely hard, store the biscuits somewhere cool (if stored in an airtight container, they will remain crisp for some days).

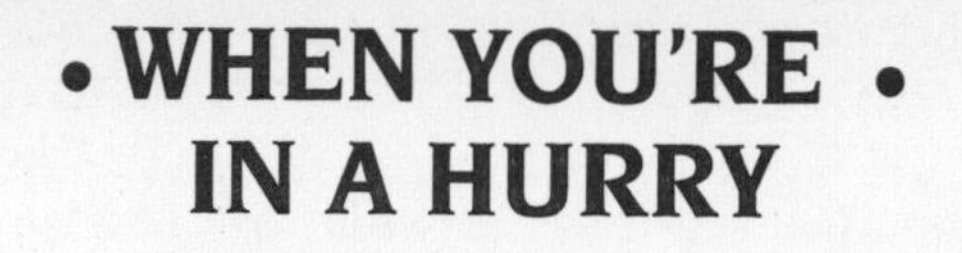

• WHEN YOU'RE • IN A HURRY

If you come in late and want a meal immediately, a pasta dish is about as near instant as you can get. A variety of dishes based on tagliolini or tagliatelle, spaghetti(ni) or noodles can be prepared and cooked in only a few minutes. Two of the following recipes take only as long as the water takes to boil and the pasta to cook, and the others not much more.

Do not think, just because the following dishes are simple and quick, that they are in any way second-best: they are all as well worth serving when you are not in a hurry as any others in this book. However, the maxim holds good that the simpler the sauce, the more the pasta counts. When you have more time, you will find that it pays even more than usual to make the tagliatelle for the Gorgonzola sauce, in particular, yourself.

• Tagliatelle with Creamy • Gorgonzola Sauce

This is not particularly economical, since it calls for both Gorgonzola and (single) cream, but it is impossible to regret a single penny of the cost (also it is worth all the cholesterol).

I have tried making the sauce with Stilton, which is cheaper, but the result is a waste of cheese: a passable substitute for Gorgonzola is dolcelatte, which, however, is even more expensive.

Altogehter, the dish takes less than 10 minutes to prepare and cook.

Use unflavoured tagliatelle: the sauce needs no embellishment. *For* 2.

• INGREDIENTS •

250 *g*/9 *oz plain tagliatelle*	40 *g*/1 1/2 *oz pecorino*
125 *g*/4 1/2 *oz Gorgonzola*	142 *ml*/1/4 *pint carton single cream*
25 *g*/1 *oz butter*	*Salt*

Large saucepan
Sharp knife
Grater
Wok or small frying-pan
Spatula
Colander or sieve

• METHOD •

1 Set the water for the pasta to boil. Chop or crumble the Gorgonzola into small pieces; roughly chop the butter. Finely grate the pecorino if necessary.

2 Start cooking the tagliatelle (see pages 50–1). Pour the cream into a wok or smallish frying-pan (preferably a wok), bring to the boil over medium heat, and allow to boil for 1 minute or until reduced by about a third. Remove from the heat and instantly add the butter, Gorgonzola, and a little salt. Stir until the cheese has melted and the sauce is smooth, if necessary pressing the lumps of cheese gently against the bottom of the pan.

3 Thoroughly drain the pasta and immediately toss with the pecorino. Add and toss in the sauce. Serve at once.

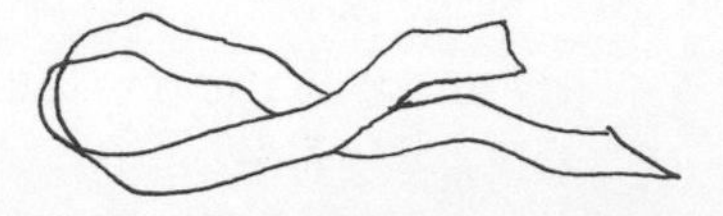

• TAGLIATELLE WITH • LEMON SAUCE AND PECORINO

To lovers of cheesecake, the combination of lemon and cheese may not be unexpected, but the interest and depth of flavour produced by the unsweetened lemon and pecorino are nevertheless surprising.

You can make the sauce in two ways, either using soft cheese or single cream: the soft cheese version is thicker (and more nutritious) but costs more and calls for a smooth-textured, fresh-tasting cheese (Italian ricotta is ideal in terms of flavour but sometimes disintegrates into curds when mixed with the pasta).

As the skin of the lemon as well as the juice is needed, the lemon should be fresh: the skin of lemons kept for a long time becomes tough and withered and is difficult to grate.

Ideally, use fresh (bought or home-made) plain, tomato or spinach tagliatelle.

With either method, the sauce takes only as long to prepare and cook as the pasta to boil.

Serve with extra pecorino. *For 2.*

WITH SOFT CHEESE

• INGREDIENTS •

250 g/9 oz tagliatelle

40 g/1 ½ oz pecorino

1 lemon

About 2 tablespoonsful milk

200 g/7 oz smooth, fresh-tasting medium-fat soft cheese

Salt

Hot chilli powder

Pepper

Large saucepan
Grater

Fork
Bowl
Colander or sieve

• METHOD •

1 Set the water to boil for the pasta. Finely grate the pecorino if necessary. Wash and dry the lemon. Finely grate the zest (the yellow surface of the skin); then squeeze.
2 Start cooking the pasta (see pages 50–1). In a bowl, beat the milk gradually into the cheese until smooth. The amount you need varies according to the cheese: use enough to give the consistency of thick cream. Stir in a little salt, a large pinch of chilli powder, the lemon zest, and 4 teaspoonsful of juice.
3 Drain the pasta and toss immediately first with the pecorino, then with the sauce. Add a moderate sprinkling of pepper; serve extra pecorino and the rest of the lemon juice separately.

WITH CREAM

• INGREDIENTS •

250 g/9 oz tagliatelle
40 g/1 1/2 oz pecorino
1 lemon
142 ml/1/4 pint carton single cream
Salt
Hot chilli powder
Pepper

Large saucepan
Grater
Wok
Fork
Colander or sieve

• METHOD •

1 Set the water to boil for the pasta. Finely grate the pecorino if necessary. Wash and dry the lemon; finely grate the zest and squeeze the juice.
2 Start cooking the pasta (see pages 50–1). Pour the cream into a wok or smallish saucepan, add a little salt and a generous

pinch of chilli powder, and bring to the boil over medium heat. Allow to boil 1–1½ minutes or until thick and reduced by about a third. Remove from the heat.

3 Drain the pasta, and toss immediately with the pecorino. Stir the lemon zest and 4 teaspoonsful of the lemon juice into the cream. Toss with the pasta and add a sprinkling of pepper. Accompany the dish with more pecorino and the rest of the lemon juice.

• Spaghetti with Ham • and Sun-dried Tomatoes

Sun-dried tomatoes are expensive but (like porcini) you need only very few to make an impact. At some good Italian grocers or delicatessens you can buy them as they are, i.e. dry; otherwise, they are sold loose or in jars in olive and/or sunflower oil. Many supermarkets now stock them in oil: at the time of going to press, a 285-g jar with mixed olive and sunflower oil costs about £1.40p.

This recipe works about equally well hot or cold: if you plan to serve it cold, use only one rather than two tablespoonsful of oil for frying and add the extra tablespoonful to the pasta when cold. Conversely, toss the hot pasta with 75 g/3 oz rather than 40 g/1½ oz grated pecorino. To serve hot, accompany with extra pecorino; to serve cold, place a dollop of Home-made Soft Cheese (see page 176) on top of each portion: the moist, mild cheese offsets the pungency of the tomatoes and garlic perfectly. Either way, accompany with a green or tomato salad if possible.

The dish takes only a few minutes to prepare and 9–11 minutes (the average time that spaghetti takes) to cook. *For* 2.

• INGREDIENTS •

Bunch parsley (enough for 3 tablespoonsful when chopped)

4 cloves garlic

50 g/2 oz sliced ham, preferably smoked

25 g/1 oz sun-dried tomatoes

40 g/1 1/2 oz pecorino cheese (or 75 g/3 oz for serving cold)

250 g/9 oz spaghetti

2 tablespoonsful olive oil (use only 1 for frying if serving cold)

Sharp knife
Kitchen paper
Grater
Large saucepan
Frying-pan
Spatula
Colander or sieve
Tablespoon

• METHOD •

1 Trim the ends of the parsley stalks; wash and blot dry with kitchen paper, and chop finely. Peel and finely chop the garlic. Remove any fat from the ham and dice; dice the tomatoes. Keep all the ingredients separate. Finely grate the pecorino if necessary. Set the water to boil for the pasta.

2 Start cooking the spaghetti (see pages 50–1). Heat the oil over fairly high heat 3 minutes before you expect it to be ready. Add the garlic and allow to fry until light brown. Add the tomatoes and stir-fry for 1/2 minute. Add the ham and stir-fry for another 1/2 minute. Stir in the parsley and remove from the heat.

3 Drain the pasta and toss with the pecorino. Add and toss in the other ingredients.

4 Serve hot with extra pecorino or cold with extra olive oil and a generous spoonful of home-made cheese.

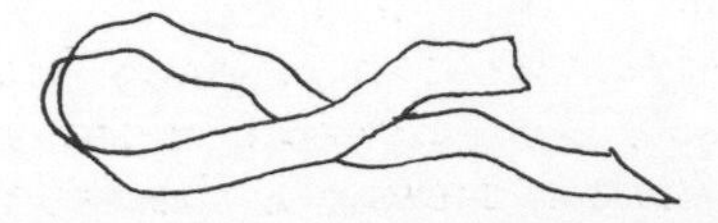

• TAGLIATELLE WITH • HAM AND CHEESE SAUCE

This takes about 5 minutes to prepare and 10 minutes to cook. As the heat of the pasta helps to melt the cheese in the sauce, this is one of the cases where you definitely should toss the sauce into the pasta before serving.

The quantities given are for 3: if there are only 2 of you, make the full quantity of sauce and keep the spare portion as a sandwich filling: it is delicious cold.

Obviously, being in a hurry precludes making your own pasta, but if you serve the dish at other times or have some already, use home-made tomato, maize or spinach tagliatelle; or buy a packet of mixed plain, spinach, and tomato. *For* 3.

• INGREDIENTS •

1 *medium to large onion*

125 *g*/4½ *oz sliced smoked ham*

50 *g*/2 *oz pecorino cheese*

About 2 *tablespoonsful milk*

200 *g*/7 *oz smooth medium-fat soft cheese*

15 *g*/½ *oz butter*

½ *tablespoonful olive oil*

375 *g*/13 *oz tagliatelle*

Pepper

Sharp knife
Grater
Bowl
Fork
Frying-pan
Large saucepan

• METHOD •

1 Peel and finely chop the onion. Finely dice the ham, removing any fat. Grate the pecorino if necessary. Beat the milk gradually into the soft cheese: as cheeses vary, you may not

need quite this amount. The aim is to bring it to the consistency of thick cream. Stir in the pecorino.

2 Melt the butter in the oil over fairly low heat; add the onion and fry for 8–10 minutes, stirring often, until soft but not brown. While the onion cooks, set the water to boil for the pasta. Start cooking the pasta (see pages 50–1) when the onion is soft.

3 Add the ham to the onion and cook for 1–2 minutes. Remove from the heat and stir in the cheese. Leave off the heat until the pasta is drained. Return the pasta to the hot saucepan, put the cheese sauce over the heat just until the cheese starts to melt, which will be for only a moment or two, and immediately add and toss with the pasta in the saucepan. Season with a little pepper and serve at once.

• Noodles with Bacon • and Beansprouts

This is one of the quickest possible stir-fried dishes: it is designed to entail the minimum of chopping up, and, because of their crispness, the accompanying ingredients go much better with boiled than fried noodles. For instructions on how to grow your own beansprouts, see page 185. *For 2–3.*

• INGREDIENTS •

200 g/7 oz mung beansprouts

50 g/2 oz mange-tout or sugar-snap peas

2 large sticks celery

2-cm/3/4-inch piece root ginger

2 cloves garlic

125 g/4 1/2 oz bacon

250 g/9 oz noodles

2 tablespoonsful groundnut oil

2 1/2 teaspoonsful light soy sauce

Sieve
2 plates
Kitchen paper

Sharp knife
Scissors
Large saucepan
Wok or frying-pan

• METHOD •

1 Carefully pick over the beansprouts; wash, shake in a sieve to remove surplus moisture, and spread out on a plate lined with kitchen paper to dry. Wash the peas, trim the ends, and cut diagonally into 1-cm/1/3-inch slices. Put on another plate lined with kitchen paper. Trim the leaf and root ends of the celery and remove any discoloured streaks: wash, dry, and slice finely. Place on the plate with the peas. Peel and finely slice the ginger and garlic, removing any fibrous patches on the ginger. Trim the rind from the bacon and cut into 1-cm/1/3-inch squares (use scissors).

2 Set the water to boil for the noodles. Time them to allow 5 minutes for stir-frying the other ingredients. Check that all the vegetables are dry; if necessary, blot with kitchen paper. Set all the prepared ingredients and the soy sauce conveniently to hand near the cooker. Warm the oil in a wok or frying-pan over high heat. Add the garlic and ginger and allow to fry until just beginning to change colour. Add the beansprouts and bacon and stir-fry for 2 1/2 minutes. Add the celery and peas and stir-fry for 2–2 1/2 minutes, until the bacon is just crisp. Add the soy sauce, stir, and remove from the heat.

3 Drain the noodles, distribute into serving-bowls, and place the stir-fried ingredients on top.

• WHEN YOU'RE • REALLY BROKE

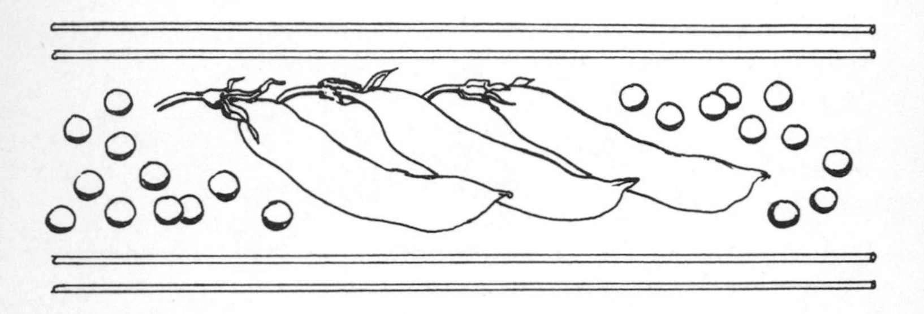

Many of the dishes in other parts of the book are very cheap, notably Parsley Pesto (see page 65) and Yoghurt Soup (page 32), which (without accompaniments) calls only for pasta, yoghurt and spices. Spaghetti with Mushroom Sauce and Basil Butter and Tuna Fish and Chilli Salad (pages 70 and 134) are fairly cheap. And will you not find many dishes which cost less than pasta with Plum Tomato Sauce (400 g/14 oz tins of plum tomatoes normally cost about 30p but can sometimes be bought as special offers for very much less). You can also have a bargain gourmet meal if you make ravioli filled with Clara's Cheese and Potato Stuffing (page 104) accompanied by Parsley Pesto (rather than Olive and Tomato Sauce, although even this – if made with plum tomatoes – is fairly economical).

I have given a selection of more very cheap dishes here, including Pea and Pecorino Soup with Ditali (page 171) and Macaroni Cheese (page 185). There is also a recipe for Pasta Pancakes (page 173), which are an attractive way of using up left-over pasta. To go with them, I have suggested making your own soft cheese. Similarly, to go with Kumud's Hot Macaroni with Beansprouts (page 183), I have given directions for growing your own mung beans, which halves the cost of the sprouts. If the situation is really dire, you can resort simply to spaghetti with garlic and pecorino – but do not omit the pecorino.

• Pea and Pecorino • Soup with Ditali

In my house, this soup is known as 'Rainy Summer Soup' beacause, with the green peas and cabbage, it looks very summery but is at the same time warming and satisfying on a wet day.

It is extremely cheap: apart from the ditali, the only item which you are likely to have to buy specially is the peas (use fresh ones if at all possible).

You may have to go to a pasta shop for ditali, but you can use thin-cut macaroni instead.

Up to the addition of the pasta, the soup can be prepared several hours in advance; once completed, however, it should be eaten promptly, since not only will the pasta swell if it is left standing (see page 31), but the cabbage will become soggy.

Serve alone, with extra pecorino or with Parsley Butter (see page 76), and accompany with crusty bread. *For* 3–4.

• INGREDIENTS •

750 g/1 lb 8 oz fresh peas (or 375 g/13 oz frozen)

Salt

1 chicken or vegetable stock-cube

2 largish onions

1 stick celery

1 small potato (any sort)

4 leaves of a green cabbage

1 pepper-shaped or 1/2 a pod-shaped green chilli

1 tablespoonful oil

15 g/1/2 oz butter

2 teaspoonsful white flour

1 pint milk

50 g/2 oz pecorino

75 g/3 oz ditali

Saucepan
Sharp knife
Grater (optional)

• METHOD •

1 Shell the peas. Just cover with slightly salted water and boil 5–9 minutes or until tender. Drain over a bowl; keep the cooking-liquor.

2 Measure the liquor (use a mug if necessary) and dissolve the stock-cube in as much of the boiling water as will make up 600 ml/1 pint when added to it; when it has fully dissolved, add the liquor.

3 Peel and finely chop the onions. Trim the leaf and root ends of the celery; pare off any discoloured streaks, wash, dry, and dice into pea-sized pieces. Peel the potato and dice into similarly small pieces. Wash the cabbage leaves, cut out any thick stalks, and shred. Wash, dry, and halve the chilli; wrap the half of a long one, which you will not need, in foodwrap and store in the refrigerator. Remove the stalk end, inner membrane, and all the seeds and dice as finely as possible. Do not touch your eyes while handling it and wash your hands directly afterwards.

4 Fry the onion and celery in the oil and butter over low heat 8–10 minutes, turning often; add the chilli and potato and fry 3–5 minutes more, or until the onion is soft but not brown. Stir in the flour. Add the milk and bring to a simmer. Add the stock, return to the simmer, and simmer 10 minutes. If you are making the soup in advance, remove from the heat until it is needed and cover; put the prepared cabbage (also covered) into the refrigerator.

5 Grate the cheese if necessary. If the soup was made in advance up to this point, bring it back to a simmer. Check the cooking time of the ditali on the packet (if given): they will probably take 10 minutes. Add and cook at just above simmering (i.e. at a very gentle boil) for 5 minutes less than the time it takes to cook. Stir in the cabbage and cook for another 4 minutes; add the peas and cook for another minute. Stir in the cheese, remove from the heat, and serve immediately.

• Using up Left-over Pasta •

• Pasta Pancakes •

Left-over pasta can be used in various ways: one of the best is as a stuffing for pancakes, which are so good that it is definitely worth cooking a couple of extra portions in order to make them. Their excellence is due to the fact that the batter contains less flour than usual, giving a particularly light, crisp result which contrasts with the smoothness of the pasta. I originally tried these proportions after reading Marcella Hazan's *The Classic Italian Cookbook* and, although this sort of batter especially suits pasta, have used it for pancakes with stuffings of all kinds ever since.

Almost any sort of pasta is suitable for a stuffing: I have tried spaghetti, bucatini, tagliatelle, macaroni, and rigatoni. If the pasta is plain or tossed only with Parmesan or pecorino, add Parsley Butter (see page 76) or mix it with Home-made Soft Cheese (page 176), plus a sprinkling of more Parmesan or pecorino; if it is tossed with sauce, add only Parmesan or pecorino.

A sauce to serve with the pancakes is not essential, but if they are stuffed with pasta mixed only with cheeses or tossed in a tomato-based sauce, an accompaniment of Plum Tomato Sauce (page 53) is an improvement. Depending on the stuffing, you could make the sauce with half a chilli (add the finely chopped chilli 5 minutes after the garlic) or mix 2–3 table-spoonsful of chopped parsley into it just before serving.

The batter can be made up to 24 hours in advance. You can either eat the pancakes at once, as soon as they are fried, or fry them in advance and re-heat them: to re-heat a full quantity, however, will call for a large baking-tray or a very large ovenware dish (see page 175).

With bulky pasta such as rigatoni, you may have difficulty in folding the pancakes tidily: I have no especial remedy to offer, but merely warn you.

The following quantity makes 24 tablespoonsful of batter, which I have suggested making into 8 large pancakes. However, their size will depend on the width of your pan, since it is important that the batter should just cover the bottom thinly. A wok, because of its smaller flat base, is not ideal for pancake-making, but the size I have given can be cooked fairly successfully in a large one.

Allow at least 30 minutes for the batter to rest. *For* 4.

PANCAKES

• INGREDIENTS •

100 *g*/3½ *oz plain white flour*

Salt

2 *size*-2 *eggs*

250 *ml/scant* ½ *pint milk*

4–5 *tablespoonsful oil, preferably olive, plus* 1 *teaspoonful*

Parmesan or pecorino for sprinkling (optional)

FILLING

• INGREDIENTS •

200–220 *g*/7 *oz cooked pasta*

FOR PLAIN PASTA OR PASTA TOSSED ONLY WITH CHEESE:

Parsley Butter (see page 76), *or* 200 *g*/7 *oz Home-made Soft Cheese (page* 176)

40–50 *g*/1½ *oz Parmesan or pecorino*

FOR PASTA TOSSED IN SAUCE:

A sprinkling of Parmesan or pecorino

Fish-slice
Frying-pan
Mixing bowl
Tablespoon
Teaspoon

Cloth or plate
Small saucepan (for Parsley Butter)
Grater
Kitchen paper

FOR RE-HEATING THE PANCAKES:

Aluminium foil
Baking-tray at least 30 cm/12 inches square or shallow ovenware dish of similar area, e.g. 40 cm/16 inches × 25 cm/10 inches

• METHOD •

1 Mix the flour with a fairly generous pinch of salt and make a well in the middle. Wash, dry, and break in the eggs. Stir them gradually into the flour, starting with the flour on the inside of the well and working outwards. When all the flour is incorporated, add 1 teaspoonful olive oil, and then add and stir in the milk by degrees, pressing out any lumps against the side of the bowl. Continue to stir until the mixture is smooth. Cover and leave for 30 minutes. (If you wish to leave it overnight, store in the refrigerator.) After leaving it to stand, beat thoroughly with a fork before use. Make Plum Tomato Sauce if you plan to serve it; do not start frying the pancakes until it is ready.

2 Mix plain pasta with Home-made Soft Cheese or make Parsley Butter. The cheese is fairly stiff: if it is very difficult to mix, soften it with just a very little milk (or cream). Gently melt Parsley Butter in a small saucepan and toss the pasta into it.

3 Grate the Parmesan or pecorino if necessary and set near the cooker with the batter, the prepared filling, and either serving-plates or the dish or tray for re-heating the pancakes; line a tray with aluminium foil. Put 1 tablespoonful of oil into the frying-pan and warm briefly over moderate heat. Add 3 tablespoonsful of batter and immediately tip the pan to spread it over the bottom. Allow to fry until the underside is golden: lift it at the edges to see when it is ready. Slide the fish-slice underneath it, quickly turn it over, and fry the second side, which will not take as long as the first. As the second side cooks, place 1 heaped tablespoonful of pasta to one side of it, leaving a wide margin at the edges. Sprinkle the filling with Parmesan or pecorino and

as soon as the second side is golden, fold or roll it up. Lift it carefully on to a serving-plate or the tray or dish with the fish-slice. Remove the pan from the heat for a moment to cool it (if it is very hot, the batter for the next pancake may set before it has spread). Remove any fragments of filling or batter. There should be enough oil to fry the next pancake, but if the pan is dry, add a little more. Return it to the heat, add another 3 tablespoonsful of batter, and proceed as before. Continue until the batter is finished; add another tablespoonful of oil after every second pancake plus just a little extra if needed.
4 Either eat straight away with sauce (if you are serving it) and/or grated Parmesan or pecorini, or re-heat the pancakes, which can be left for several hours: cover with foodwrap or a clean cloth or put into the (cold) oven until needed. When you wish to eat them, pre-heat the oven to 180°C, 350°F, Gas Mark 4, and bake 12–14 minutes; serve as above.

• Home-made Soft Cheese •

This will save you at least 20p per 200 g/7 oz, but I recommend it less for the sake of economy than for its mild, fresh yet rich flavour. As it is a curd cheese rather than homogenous, it is not a satisfactory substitute for smooth cheese in sauces and elsewhere, nor does it have enough flavour to use in the recipes as they stand for Ravioli and Cannelloni fillings; however, it is ideal for moistening pasta in pancakes and as an alternative to cottage cheese for sandwiches and snacks.

It is extremely easy to make: all that it involves is simmering the milk and allowing it to drain.

To drain it, you will need the equivalent of cheese-cloth. For this, I suggest a disposable paper cleaning-cloth: it should be new for the cheese, but it can be rinsed and used for cleaning afterwards. *Makes 200 g/7 oz.*

• INGREDIENTS •

1.2 litres/2 pints whole (i.e. unskimmed) milk

Salt

½ lemon

Large saucepan
Sieve
Paper cleaning-cloth

• METHOD •

1 Rinse a large saucepan with cold water (this helps to prevent the milk from catching on the bottom) and pour in the milk. Squeeze the lemon and add 1 tablespoonful of the juice. Sprinkle in a fairly generous pinch of salt, stir, and bring to the boil: watch to ensure that it does not boil over (as there will be curds on the top, you may not see it bubbling). Adjust the heat to a simmer and simmer for 15 minutes.
2 Drain through a sieve lined with the cloth for about 2 hours.
3 Season with sea-salt to taste.

The cheese will keep in the refrigerator for up to 2 days.

• Pasta Omelette •

This is a more expensive way than pancakes of using up pasta, because you will need two eggs each rather than two altogether. On the other hand, it has the advantage of being almost instant. As with pancakes, virtually any sort of pasta, dressed or otherwise, can be used; if it is plain, I suggest adding Parmesan or pecorino and Parsley Butter (see page 76); if tossed with tomato or other sauce, it will need only a sprinkling of Parmesan or pecorino.

Serve with crusty bread and if possible crudities, e. g. carrots, celery and/or green pepper. Scrub or peel carrots, chop into shortish lengths, and cut into strips (stand the lengths on end and cross-chop). Trim the root and leaf ends of celery and wash (with inner sticks, you may prefer to leave the leaves, which are decorative, untrimmed). Wash and quarter a pepper, remove the white inner membrane and seeds, and slice. *For 2.*

• INGREDIENTS •

4 size-2 eggs
Salt
If the pasta is plain, 1/2 quantity Parsley Butter (see page 76)

Pepper

About 15 g/½ oz Parmesan or pecorino

About ½ an average portion of plain or dressed cooked pasta (i.e. 50 g/2 oz uncooked)

1 tablespoonful oil

Extra Parmesan or pecorino for sprinkling (optional)

Large bowl
Fork
Grater (optional)
Large frying-pan or wok
Fish-slice

• Method •

1 Wash, dry, and break the eggs into a bowl. Season moderately with salt and pepper and beat with a fork until smooth. Grate the Parmesan or pecorino if necessary.

2 Set the serving-plates, pasta, grated cheese, and parsley butter (if you are using it) within easy reach of the cooker. Warm the oil in the wok or frying-pan over medium heat; tip a wok (unless it is non-stick) to give it a coating a little way up the sides. Add the egg and tilt the wok or pan so that it runs in a thin layer over the bottom. As soon as it starts to set, fold the set part back towards the middle. Tip the pan again so that more liquid egg runs over the bottom; fold it back and repeat until all the egg at the bottom is set. Add the pasta, parsley butter, and a sprinkling of Parmesean or pecorino and continue to cook until the egg at the top has set and the underneath of the omelette is golden (to check, lift it with the fish-slice at one side). Fold it in two, sprinkle with a little extra cheese if you wish, and remove from the heat. Cut it in half and serve immediately.

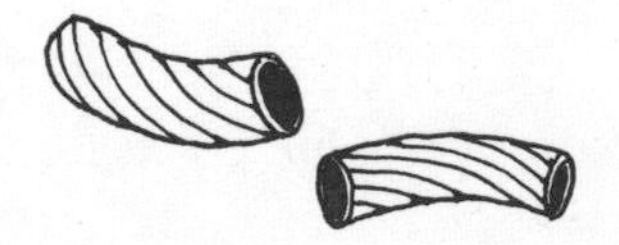

• Spaghetti with • Garlic and Chilli

This is one of the cheapest possible ways of serving spaghetti. Its character depends on the garlic slices, which should be fried to crisp brown chips.

I have given two tablespoonsful of oil because without sauce the spaghetti would otherwise be dry.

Serve with plenty of extra pecorino. *For* 2.

• INGREDIENTS •

Bunch parsley (enough for 3 tablespoonsful when chopped)

4–6 *cloves garlic*

40 *g*/1½ *oz pecorino*

½ *green chilli*

250 *g*/9 *oz spaghetti*

Salt

2 *tablespoonsful olive oil*

Sharp knife
Kitchen paper
Grater
Large saucepan
Wok or frying-pan
Colander

• METHOD •

1 Trim the bottoms of the parsley stalks; wash the parsley, blot dry with kitchen paper, and chop finely. Peel and finely slice the garlic. Grate the pecorino if necessary. Wash, dry, and halve the chilli (wrap the half you do not need in foodwrap and store in the refrigerator). Pinch the stalk end from the half to be used, remove the inner membrane and all the seeds, and dice as finely as possible. Do not rub your eyes while handling it and wash your hands afterwards.

2 Boil the spaghetti in plenty of salted water. Three minutes before you expect it to be ready, heat the oil in a wok or frying-pan over high heat. Add the garlic and allow it to fry until starting to change colour. Add the chilli and continue to fry until the garlic is golden brown. Stir in the parsley and remove from the heat.

3 Drain the spaghetti, return it to the saucepan, and immediately toss with the pecorino. Add and toss in the contents of the frying-pan. Serve at once with more grated pecorino.

• Spaghetti or Capricciosa • with Peas and Chilli

This is one of those perfect recipes that is both cheap and quick – and does not merit being served only when you are broke. At times when you are not broke, use fresh capricciosa – plain, flavoured or mixed.

You may find that you do not want extra pecorino with this dish, but have some ready in case you do. *For* 2.

• INGREDIENTS •

500 *g*/1 *lb* 2 *oz fresh or* 250 *g*/9 *oz frozen peas*

Salt

2 *medium onions*

1/2 *green or (preferably) yellow chilli*

250 *g*/9 *oz spaghetti or capricciosa*

2 *tablespoonsful olive oil*

40 *g*/1 1/2 *oz pecorino cheese*

Saucepan
Sharp knife
Grater (optional)
Frying-pan
Sieve or colander

• METHOD •

1 Shell the fresh peas; just cover with slightly salted water and boil for 5–9 minutes, until tender. Cook frozen peas for as long as directed on the packet. If there is much cooking water left, drain over a bowl and add the liquor to the water in which you cook the pasta.

2 Peel and chop the onion. Wash, dry and halve the chilli. (Wrap the half you do not need in foodwrap and store in the refrigerator.) Pinch the stalk end from the half to be used, remove the seeds and inner membrane, and dice as finely as possible. Do not rub your eyes while handling the chilli, and wash your hands directly afterwards. Finely grate the pecorino if necessary.

3 Set the water to boil for the pasta. Put in the pasta, allowing 12 minutes for cooking the onion and chilli. Add slightly less salt to the water than usual if it contains pea liquor. Fry the onions in the oil over a fairly low heat for 8–10 minutes or until soft but not brown; add the chilli and fry for 2 minutes. If the pasta is not ready, remove from the heat.

4 Drain the pasta in a sieve or colander set over a bowl to catch a little of the cooking water. Toss with the pecorino. Return the onions and chilli to the heat, turn them in the oil and add 1 tablespoonful of the hot pasta-water. Toss them into the pasta and serve at once, with more grated pecorino if needed.

• Stir-Fried Noodles with Egg •

In this recipe the noodles are not fried crisp, as for chow mein, but are stir-fried relatively quickly to amalgamate them with the egg. Although by no means the same, the dish bears some resemblance to a more elaborate version demonstrated to me by the Thai cook Supasri Gilbert.

Use very fresh eggs and fresh peas when possible.

Although three of the ingredients need boiling before frying, in terms of working-time the dish is quick to prepare.

Allow an hour for the noodles to dry. *For* 2–3.

• INGREDIENTS •

250 *g*/9 *oz chow mein or other noodles*

2 *cloves garlic*

1/2 *pod-shaped green chilli*

250 g/9 oz cabbage

Salt

375 g/13 oz fresh peas (or 190 g/6½ oz frozen)

1 large or 1½ medium onions

1.5 cm/½ inch piece root ginger

3 eggs (any size)

Pepper

5 tablespoonsful groundnut oil

5 teaspoonsful light soy sauce

Large saucepan
Fork or chopsticks
Colander or sieve
Plate
Kitchen paper
Sharp knife
Small bowl
Wok or large frying-pan

• METHOD •

1 Boil the noodles as directed on the packet; separate them as they cook with a fork or chopsticks. Be careful not to overcook them. Drain in a colander, rinse under the cold tap to remove surplus starch, and leave in the colander for an hour to dry.

2 Peel off the outermost leaves of the cabbage. Cut out any hard stalks, shred coarsely, and wash. Bring about 600 ml/1 pint slightly salted water to the boil; put in the cabbage, bring back to the boil, and boil briskly for 2 minutes. Drain in a sieve, rinse under the cold tap, and leave on a plate lined with kitchen paper to dry (do not leave in the sieve, since you will need it for the peas).

3 Shell the peas. Peel and dice (rather than finely chop) the onion; peel and finely slice the ginger and garlic, discarding any fibrous patches on the ginger. Wash, dry and halve the chilli; wrap the half you will not need in foodwrap and store in the refrigerator. Trim the stalk end of the part to be used, remove the inner membrane and seeds, and slice finely. Do not rub your eyes while handling it and wash your hands immediately afterwards.

4 Just cover the peas with slightly salted water, bring to the boil, and boil 5–9 minutes, until tender. Drain and return to the hot saucepan; cover with a plate or lid to keep them warm.

5 Wash, dry, and break the eggs into a smallish bowl; season moderately with salt and pepper and beat until smooth with a fork. Check to ensure that the noodles and cabbage are dry; loosen the noodles with a fork. Set all the prepared ingredients plus serving bowls and the soy sauce conveniently to hand near the cooker. Warm 2 tablespoonsful of the oil in the wok or frying-pan over high heat. Add the garlic and ginger and fry until just beginning to change colour. Add the chilli and stir. Add the onion and stir-fry 1 minute; add the cabbage and stir-fry for another minute. Remove from the heat and transfer, including the ginger and garlic, to a plate (you can use the one on which the cabbage was drying, but remove the damp kitchen-paper). Wipe the wok or frying-pan, add 2 more tablespoonsful of oil, and return to the heat. Allow to warm briefly, and pour in the egg. Tilt the pan to spread it, and as soon as it starts to set at the bottom, add the noodles and stir. Stir-fry until the pan is completely dry, which means that the egg is cooked. Add 3 teaspoonsful of the soy sauce, remove from the heat, and distribute into the serving-bowls. Put the remaining tablespoonful of oil into the wok and allow to heat. Return the vegetables to it and stir-fry 1/2–1 minute. Add the peas and stir-fry for a few seconds. Stir in the remaining 2 teaspoonsful of soy sauce and place on top of the noodles. Serve at once.

• Kumud's Hot Macaroni • with Beansprouts

Be warned: this is (and should be) decidedly hot: to cool it, serve with yoghurt or yoghurt and cucumber salad, if possible with mint.

It is cheap even if you use ready-sprouted beans, but cheaper still if you sprout your own: this is very easy (see page 185) but you need to allow 3 days.

Apart from sprouting the beans, the dish is quick to prepare and takes only as long to cook as the macaroni plus 4–4 1/2 minutes for stir-frying. *For* 3.

• INGREDIENTS •

About 375 g/13 oz mung beansprouts

1 teaspoonful cumin seeds

½ teaspoonful mustard seeds

2.5-cm/1-inch piece root ginger

1 × 375-g/13-oz tin sweetcorn

1 lime

1 pod-shaped chilli

100 g/3½ oz thin-cut macaroni

2 tablespoonsful groundnut oil plus a little extra

⅓ teaspoonful turmeric

⅓ teaspoonful hot chilli powder

Teaspoon
Tablespoon
Tin-opener
Sieve
Plate
Kitchen paper
Pestle and mortar
Grater
Sharp knife
Large saucepan
Wok or large saucepan

• METHOD •

1 Pick over and thoroughly wash the beansprouts in cold water. Shake in a sieve to remove surplus moisture and spread on a plate lined with kitchen paper to dry. Crush the cumin and mustard seeds in a mortar. Peel the ginger and coarsely grate or finely chop, discarding any fibrous patches. Drain the sweetcorn. Squeeze half the lime; cut the other half into 3 wedges. Wash, dry, and slit the chilli; remove the stalk end, inner membrane, and all the seeds, and dice as finely as possible. Wash your hands directly afterwards.

2 Cook the macaroni for the shortest time directed on the packet: drain, return to saucepan, and toss in a very little oil.

3 Check that the beansprouts are dry: if necessary, blot with kitchen paper. Set all the prepared ingredients to hand plus the turmeric and hot chilli powder. Heat the remaining oil over fairly high heat in the wok or saucepan. Add the cumin and mustard and allow to fry for a few seconds. Add the ginger, chilli, and beansprouts and stir-fry 2½ minutes. Add the corn and macaroni and turn in the oil. Add the turmeric and chilli powder and stir-fry 1½–2 minutes. Add the lime juice, stir, and remove from the heat. Serve at once with the wedges of lime.

TO SPROUT MUNG BEANS

For about 375 *g*/13 *oz sprouts, you will need* 150 *g*/5 *oz beans.*

Large, shallow dish
Tea-cloth

Set the beans to soak in lukewarm water overnight. Drain and put into the dish with enough warm water to half cover them. Place a cloth over the dish to exclude light and set in a warm place, such as on top of the boiler, for two days; look at them at intervals and add a little more warm water if they become dry. You can leave them to grow for another one or two days: when you wish to stop them growing, wash in cold water and store for up to 24 hours in a sealed foodbag in the refrigerator.

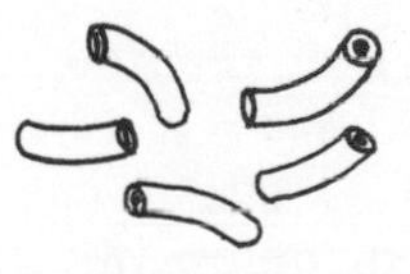

• Macaroni Cheese •

I have thought of giving a recipe for Macaroni Cheese before, but have been deterred by the general opinion that it is boring: however, I feel that it should have a place in this book as virtually the only pasta dish which can be considered traditionally British; also, if it is made with plenty of well-flavoured sauce and a crisp top, it is pleasant, if undemanding, rather than dull.

Take care to use the right amount of macaroni and avoid the quicker-cooking, thin-cut variety. Strong, mature Cheddar cheese is essential: mild Cheddar gives almost no flavour at all.

Serve with watercress, celery, or tomato salad. *For* 4.

• INGREDIENTS •

275 g/10 oz macaroni (not quick-cook)

25 g/1 oz stale bread (brown or white)

250 g/9 oz mature Cheddar cheese

50 g/2 oz butter

600 ml/1 pint milk

40 g/1 1/2 oz plain white flour

Salt

Pepper

2 teaspoonsful mild French mustard such as Grey Poupon, or 1 teaspoonful stronger mustard such as Dijon

Large saucepan
Sharp knife
Grater
Colander or sieve
Saucepan or frying-pan
Spatula
Ovenware dish about 22 cm/9 inches across and 10 cm/4 inches deep

• METHOD •

1 Set the water to boil for the macaroni. Cut any hard crust from the bread and coarsely grate. Grate the cheese.

2 Start cooking the macaroni: boil for the shortest time given on the packet or until only just tender (see pages 50–1). Drain and toss in 15 g/1/2 oz of the butter.

3 While the macaroni cooks, heat but do not boil the milk. Melt 40 g/1 1/2 oz butter over low heat in (another) saucepan or frying-pan. Add the flour and stir until amalgamated: be careful not to let it brown. Pour in the milk slowly, stirring continuously. Continue to stir until the sauce is thick. Season generously with salt and pepper, add the mustard, and simmer 2–3 minutes, stirring constantly. Remove from the heat. Stir in three-quarters of the cheese.

4 Set the oven to 200°C, 400°F, Gas Mark 6. Grease the ovenware dish. Toss the cooked macaroni with about three quarters of the cheese sauce and turn into the dish. Cover with the rest of the sauce. Mix the remaining cheese with the breadcrumbs and sprinkle in an even layer over the top. Bake uncovered 20–25 minutes or until the top is golden and crisp. Leave for 4–5 minutes before serving.

• Using up Left-over Egg-whites •

• Spiced Lemon and • Walnut Meringue Biscuits

If you are left with two spare egg-whites after making Rich Egg Pasta (see page 18), you may like to use them for the following, which are very crisp and light and go admirably with either Michael's Orange Salad or Mango and Kiwi Fruit Salad (pages 155 and 150 respectively); or you can eat them alone, or sandwiched with whipped cream.

Hazelnuts can be used instead of walnuts, and in fact they are perhaps even better. I have given preference to walnuts only because they are cheaper.

If filled with cream, the biscuits should be eaten at once, partly because the filling will cause them to become soggy. Otherwise, they will stay crisp for several days; store in an airtight container. *Makes 24–26 small biscuits or 12–13 pairs.*

• INGREDIENTS •

50 g/2 oz walnuts or hazelnuts

2 egg-whites

Salt

125 g/4½ oz caster sugar

Pinch powdered ginger

¼ teaspoonful mace

25 g/1 oz white or finely ground wholemeal flour

Zest of 1 large lemon

1 or preferably 2 large baking-sheets
Cooking-foil
Egg-whisk

Large bowl
Spoon
Grater

• METHOD •

1 Set the oven to 200°C, 400°F, Gas Mark 6. Line the baking-sheet with cooking-foil and toast walnuts 6–8 minutes, hazelnuts 10–12, or until lightly browned. Allow to cool and crush coarsely. Lower the oven to 150°C, 300°F, Gas Mark 2.
2 Add a pinch of salt to the egg-whites and whisk until they are close-textured and stiff enough to hold their shape completely. Whisk in half the sugar. Fold in the rest with a spoon; stir gently with a diagonal downward motion. Mix the spices with the flour and fold in. Wash and dry the lemon; finely grate in the lemon zest (the yellow part of the skin). Stir in the nuts. Place dessertspoonful of the mixture 4 cm/1 1/2 inches apart on the baking-sheet(s); as you will not be able to fit more than 12 to a sheet, you will have to bake the biscuits in more than one session unless you have two baking-sheets. Bake 50 minutes; leave on the cooking-foil until cold. Lift the foil off the sheet with the biscuits on it, if you wish to re-use the sheet to continue baking.

• Lemon Cream Filling •

• INGREDIENTS •

150 *ml*/1/4 *pint double cream*
40 *g*/1 1/2 *oz caster sugar*
1 1/2 *tablespoonsful lemon juice*

Large bowl
Egg-whisk

• METHOD •

Whisk the ingredients together until very stiff. Put about 3/4 dessertspoonful between each pair of biscuits.

• NUTRITION •

For good health you need energy-giving foods, proteins, a dozen different vitamins, over a score of different minerals and a limited amount of fibre. Anyone eating a varied diet that includes cereals, some animal food and fresh fruit and vegetables will almost certainly obtain enough of all of these. However, you may find the following summary useful when planning meals.

• Energy and Proteins •

You obtain energy from fat and oil, starch and sugar, or from protein, if you do not eat enough of the first three. Fats and oils are the most concentrated sources of energy. It is, however, considered undesirable for them to form more than 30 per cent of your total calorie intake. You are also advised that saturated fats should not form more than 10 per cent (i.e. about 200 kcal per day). All fats, and foods containing them, include different kinds of fat, but butter, cream and cheese contain more of the saturated type than, for instance, olive and groundnut oil. Olive oil is largely composed of mono-unsaturated fat, and groundnut oil of mono-unsaturated (about 40 per cent) and polyunsaturated (about 30 per cent). Except for people with a particular weight problem, the amount of cholesterol that you eat is relatively unimportant.

Proteins, which are made up of various proportions and arrangements of amino acids, are essential for the growth and maintenance of body tissue. The proteins in animal produce are more accessible to humans than those in plants: for the plant variety to give comparable value, several sorts of protein must be eaten at the same time.

According to the Department of Health's *Dietary Reference Values for Food, Energy, and Nutrients in the United Kingdom* (1991), estimated average daily needs for energy and protein are:

	Kcal	Protein
18-year-olds		
Boys	2,755	46g
Girls	2,110	37g
19–49-year-olds		
Men	2,550	44g
Women	1,940	36g

However, individual requirements vary and some people will need more. To be certain of obtaining enough protein, the recommended amounts for the 19–49 age group are: men, 55g; women, 45g.

To give some idea of how this translates into meals, an average portion of hard (i.e. eggless) pasta accompanied by tomato sauce made according to the Fresh Tomato Sauce recipe on page 51 and by 25g/1oz pecorino cheese will give you just over 500kcal, plus a total of about 22g protein, 10 of which will be of animal origin and hence high value. If the pasta were egg pasta, the amount of high-value protein would be raised to about 17g.

• Vitamins •

Vitamin A is needed for healthy skin and hair; the B group of vitamins for metabolizing various food constituents; vitamin C to promote healing and prevent scurvy; and vitamin D to maintain levels of phosphorus and potassium in the blood. Good sources of Vitamin A include eggs, butter, margarine, lettuce and carrots; of the B vitamins, liver, kidneys, eggs, cheese and soya products; of vitamin C, green peppers, blackcurrants, citrus fruit and strawberries. People leading normal lives will obtain sufficient vitamin D from sunlight.

• Minerals •

The major minerals needed by the body are: iron, calcium, phosphorus, magnesium, sodium and chlorine, and potassium. In particular, iron can be obtained from liver and kidneys, eggs, watercress, chocolate and cornflakes; calcium from milk, cheese, yoghurt, flour, watercress and dried figs; phosphorus and magnesium from milk, cheese, eggs, meat and peanuts. Magnesium is also gained from vegetable produce; sodium and potassium from milk, eggs, meat, bread and, in the case of sodium, salty foods such as streaky bacon and soy sauce.

• Fibre •

Fibre is supplied by plant cellulose. Obviously, whole-grain foods will give you more than those that are refined, but excessive amounts of fibre are not recommended.

CHART OF FOOD VALUES

Figures from the *Manual of Nutrition* (HMSO, 9th edition, 1985) except where marked *

Per 100 g	Energy kcal	Protein g	Fat g	Carbo g
MEAT				
Bacon (grilled)	393	28.1	31.2	0
Beef (minced, stewed)	229	23.1	15.2	0
Chicken (roast, with skin)	213	24.4	12.8	0
Chicken (roast, without skin)	148	24.8	5.4	0
Ham	166	16.4	11.1	0
Pork chop (cooked, with fat)	332	28.5	24.2	0
FISH				
Cod, haddock, plaice	77	17.1	0.9	0
Prawns	107	22.6	1.8	0
Tuna fish (in oil)	289	22.8	22.0	0

DAIRY PRODUCE				
Eggs	147	12.3	10.9	0
Milk (whole)	65	3.2	3.9	4.6
Milk (skimmed)	32	3.4	0.1	4.7
Cream (single)	195	2.4	19.3	3.2
Cream (double)	447	1.5	48.2	2.0
Cheddar cheese	406	26.0	33.5	0
*Cream cheese**	439	3.1	47.4	tr
*Parmesan**	408	35.1	29.7	tr
*Pecarino**	536	39.6	41.9	0.1
*Ricotta**	185	10.0	14.8	2.6
Butter	740	0.4	82.0	0

GROCERIES				
Sugar (white)	394	0	0	105.3
Flour (wholemeal)	306	12.7	2.2	62.8
Bread (wholemeal)	215	9.0	2.5	41.6
Spaghetti (raw)	342	12.0	1.8	74.1
Oil (groundnut)	56	5.2	0.5	8.3
*Oil (olive)**	823	0.1	91.4	0
Soy sauce	824	0.1	91.6	0
Tomato purée	67	6.1	tr	11.4

NUTS (SHELLED), SEEDS, AND PULSES				
Almonds	565	16.9	53.5	4.3
*Hazelnuts**	665	16.1	65.1	7.2
Peanuts	570	24.3	49.0	8.6
*Walnuts**	630	16.0	56.6	15.0
Lentils (cooked)	99	7.6	0.5	17.0
*Haricot beans**	271	21.4	1.6	45.5

VEGETABLES				
Aubergine	14	0.7	0	3.1
Cauliflower (cooked)	9	1.6	0	0.8
Celery	8	0.9	0	1.3
Courgettes (raw)	29	1.6	0.4	5.0
Cucumber	10	0.6	0.1	1.8
Lettuce	12	1.0	0.4	1.2
Mushrooms	13	1.8	0.6	0
Onion	23	0.9	0	5.2

Peas (boiled, frozen)	72	6.0	0.9	10.7
Peppers (green)	12	0.9	0	2.2
Potatoes	74	2.0	0.2	17.1
Spinach	30	5.1	0.5	1.4
Tomatoes	14	0.9	0	2.8
Watercress	14	2.9	0	0.7
*Herbs: parsley**	21	5.2	tr	tr
FRUIT				
Apples	46	0.3	0	11.9
Apricots (dried)	182	4.8	0	43.4
Bananas	76	1.1	0	19.2
Figs (dried)	213	3.6	tr	52.9
Lemon juice	7	0.3	0	1.6
Olives (in brine with stone)	103	0.9	11.0	tr
Oranges	35	0.8	0	8.5
Pears	41	0.3	0	10.6

• INDEX •